NO LO
R
D0975819
RY

Re in force ments

HEIDI GRANT

Re
in
force
ments

How to Get People to **Help** *You*

HARVARD BUSINESS REVIEW PRESS

BOSTON, MASSACHUSETTS

HBR Press Quantity Sales Discounts

Harvard Business Review Press titles are available at significant quantity discounts when purchased in bulk for client gifts, sales promotions, and premiums. Special editions, including books with corporate logos, customized covers, and letters from the company or CEO printed in the front matter, as well as excerpts of existing books, can also be created in large quantities for special needs.

For details and discount information for both print and ebook formats, contact booksales@harvardbusiness.org, tel. 800-988-0886, or www.hbr.org/bulksales.

Copyright 2018 Heidi Grant
All rights reserved
Printed in the United States of America

10 9 8 7 6 5 4 3 2 1

No part of this publication may be reproduced, stored in or introduced into a retrieval system, or transmitted, in any form, or by any means (electronic, mechanical, photocopying, recording, or otherwise), without the prior permission of the publisher. Requests for permission should be directed to permissions@hbsp.harvard.edu, or mailed to Permissions, Harvard Business School Publishing, 60 Harvard Way, Boston, Massachusetts 02163.

The web addresses referenced in this book were live and correct at the time of the book's publication but may be subject to change.

Library of Congress Cataloging-in-Publication data

Names: Halvorson, Heidi Grant-, 1973- author.
Title: Reinforcements : how to get people to help you / by Heidi Grant
    Halvorson.
Description: Boston, Massachusetts : Harvard Business Review Press, [2018]
Identifiers: LCCN 2017054355 | ISBN 9781633692350 (hardcover : alk. paper)
Subjects: LCSH: Help-seeking behavior. | Persuasion (Psychology) |
    Interpersonal communication. | Management—Psychological aspects.
Classification: LCC HM1141 .H35 2018 | DDC 153.8/52—dc23 LC record
available at https://lccn.loc.gov/2017054355
    ISBN: 9781633692350
    eISBN: 9781633692367

The paper used in this publication meets the requirements of the American National Standard for Permanence of Paper for Publications and Documents in Libraries and Archives Z39.48-1992.

Contents

Asking for
Help Is the
Worst

Chapter 1

It Makes Us Feel Bad

Raise your hand if you have ever asked for help at
work or at home.
    Raise your hand if you have ever felt shy or stupid in
doing so.
    I think I can safely assume that most of us are
waving our arms wildly.

> —Alina Tugend, "Why Is Asking for Help So
> Difficult?," *New York Times*, July 7, 2007

I actually felt as if I were going to perish.

> —Psychologist Stanley Milgram, on asking a
> subway rider for their seat

Vanessa Bohns is a professor of organizational
behavior at Cornell University who, along with
her frequent collaborator Frank Flynn at Stanford, has
spent years studying how people ask for help—or more
specifically, why they are so reluctant to do so.

Her studies often involve telling participants that they will have to approach a series of strangers and ask for a favor. These favors are generally innocuous: fill out a short survey, guide me to a particular building on campus, let me borrow your cellphone for a moment. No one is asking for large sums of money, a pint of blood, or a firstborn child. Yet, as Bohns describes it, "As soon as we tell all of our participants in these studies [what they have to do], it's palpable the sense of fear and anxiety and dread. The whole room changes. It's just like the worst thing we could ask these people to do."[1]

However bad you might think being in one of Bohns's experiments would be, they've got nothing on the 1970s "subway studies" of Stanley Milgram. (You may remember him as the controversial psychologist whose most famous studies—requiring participants to give what they believed to be life-threatening shocks to another person—forever altered our understanding of obedience to authority. Clearly, it was not pleasant to be in *any* of Milgram's experiments.)

One day, after listening to his elderly mother complain that no one on the subway had offered to give her their seat, Milgram wondered what would happen if one were to just *ask* a subway rider for their seat? So he recruited his graduate students to go find out. He told them to board crowded trains in New York City and ask individuals at random for their seat. The good news: 68 percent of people willingly gave up their seats upon request. The bad news: conducting the study was—to this day—among the worst, most traumatic experiences his students had had in their lifetimes. One student, Kathryn Krogh, a clinical psychologist, recalled feeling sick to her stomach the first time she approached a passenger. Another student (and former professor of mine), Maury Silver, managed to make the request only once: "I start to ask for the man's seat. Unfortunately, I turned so white and so faint, he jumps up and puts me in the seat."[2]

Milgram, a bit skeptical as to what all the fuss was about, decided to try asking for a seat on the subway himself. He was shocked at the extent of his own discomfort; it took him several attempts just to get the words out, so paralyzed was he with fear. "Taking the man's seat, I was overwhelmed by the need to behave in a way that would justify my request," he said. "My head sank between my knees, and I could feel my face blanching. I was not role-playing. I actually felt as if I were going to perish."[3]

Although the idea of asking for even a small amount of help makes most of us horribly uncomfortable, the truth about modern work is that we rely, more than ever, on the cooperation and support of others. No one succeeds in a vacuum, whether you are in an entry-level position or have a view from the C-suite. Cross-functional teams, agile project management techniques, and matrixed or hierarchy-minimizing organizational structures mean we're all collaborating more and having to suffer the small agony of asking people to help us on a regular basis. And I'm not just talking about getting help from your colleagues and peers; if you are a leader, you need to figure out how to elicit and coordinate helpful, supportive behavior from the people you are leading, too. Arguably, that is what management *is*.

Yet our reluctance to ask for help means we often don't get the support or the resources we need. Making matters worse, our intuitions about what should make others more likely to help are often dead wrong; our fumbling, apologetic ways of asking for assistance generally make people far *less* likely to want to help. We hate imposing on people and then inadvertently make them feel imposed upon.

There's an inherent paradox in *asking* someone for their help: while help freely and enthusiastically given makes the helper feel good, researchers have found that the emotional benefits of providing help to others disappear when people feel controlled—when they are *instructed* to help, when they believe that they *should* help, or when they feel they simply have *no choice* but to help.[4]

In other words, a sense of personal agency—that you are helping because you *want* to—is essential for reaping the psychological benefits of giving support. When you don't genuinely want to help, there's nothing in it for the helper except getting it over with as quickly and with as little effort as possible. And this simple fact—more than any other—is why I wanted to write this book.

None of us can go it alone. We all need people to support us, do favors, pick up our slack, and go to bat for us. And people *are* much more likely to help us than we realize. But in many instances, we ask for help in such a way that we make people feel controlled, rather than giving them what they need to really *want* to help us— and to make helping us rewarding.

Why shouldn't the people who help you get to walk away feeling better about themselves and better about the world? In my opinion, we owe it to them. If you are going to ask someone to use their valuable time and effort on your behalf, the least you can do is to ensure that helping you leaves them better off, not worse.

But knowing how to get people to want to give you their best—and making sure they benefit as much as possible from having helped you—is not knowledge we are born with. As you'll see in the following chapters, getting other people to eagerly do what you need in response to your request requires that you create the right environment and frame your request in such a way that others will rush gladly to your aid.

I chose to call this book *Reinforcements* because there are two senses of the word "reinforcement," and each captures something really important about seeking support.

A reinforcement is generally defined as the action or process of *strengthening*. But Google offers these two more specific subdefinitions:

1. Extra personnel sent to increase the strength of an army or similar force.

2. The process of encouraging or establishing a belief or pattern of behavior, especially by encouragement or reward.

The idea of "extra personnel" required to get the job done is really the basic need I designed this book to address. Reaching your fullest potential—professionally or personally—requires you to understand how to enlist reinforcements when you need them. For many of us, "when you need them" is literally every day.

The second notion—of reinforcement as establishing a "pattern of behavior"—is the more technical sense in which psychologists tend to use the term. B. F. Skinner famously called the use of reinforcements to make particular behaviors more likely *operant conditioning*. And while human beings don't react exactly the same way as the rats and pigeons Skinner studied in his laboratory, the general principle of operant conditioning—that certain consequences or rewards can make us more likely to want to engage in a particular behavior, like helping another person in need—is spot on.

This book is organized into three major chunks. Part I is a deep dive into why we generally hate asking for help. This is the first, and major, obstacle of seeking help: overcoming the almost universal dread of actually seeking it. You'll learn why our fear of asking for help is so misguided, specifically, when and why we underestimate the likelihood of getting the support we need. You will also learn why it is fruitless to sit back and wait for people to *offer* to help you.

In part II, I explain the right ways to ask for help, laying out techniques you can use to not only increase the odds that people will want to help you, but allow them to feel genuinely good about doing so. We'll cover the kinds of basic information people need from you to even make it possible for them to give high-quality assistance. You will learn the vital difference between *controlled helping* (when people feel, for various reasons, that they have no choice but to help you) and *autonomous helping* (when giving assistance feels authentic and unforced to the helper), and how helpers' happiness and well-being are affected by engaging in each.

In part III, we will dive into why reinforcements (the people) need reinforcements (the motivators). You will see how creating a sense of "us"—offering people a way to feel good about themselves and providing them with the means to see their help "land"—provides an essential form of reinforcement for high-quality helping. If I were a Silicon Valley–type, rather than a New York social psychologist, I'd say this section of the book is about how to get help to scale—how to reinforce the helpful behavior you want to see more of, so that the people around you become more helpful without being asked.

The hard truth is that, if you aren't getting the support you need from the people in your life, it's usually more your own fault than you realize. That may sound harsh, but we all assume our needs and motivations are more obvious than they really are, and that what we intended to say overlaps perfectly with what we actually said. Psychologists call this "the transparency illusion," and it's just that: a mirage. Chances are, you're not surrounded by unhelpful loafers—just people who have no idea that you need help or what kind of help you need. The good news? We can easily solve this problem. Armed with a little knowledge, there is hope for each of us to get the support we so critically need.

In a now-famous excerpt from a four-hour interview for the Archive of American Television, the beloved children's programming creator Fred Rogers offered advice on how to help children understand and cope with the terrible things that sometimes happen in the world: "When I was a boy and I would see scary things in the news, my mother would say to me, 'Look for the helpers. You will always find people who are helping . . . if you look for the helpers, you'll know that there's hope.'"

A beautiful sentiment that captures an even more beautiful truth—human beings are, much more than it often seems, wired to want to help and support one another. And their lives are immeasurably enriched by doing so.

Your Brain, in Real Pain

People will often go to great lengths to avoid having to ask for a favor or for help of any kind, even when their need is completely genuine. My father was one of the seemingly countless legions of men who would rather drive through an alligator-infested swamp than ask for directions back to the road, which made driving with him something of a liability in the days before everyone's phone contained Google Maps. (He would invariably claim that he had not taken a wrong turn, but had "always wanted to know what was over here.")

To understand why asking for help can feel so painful, it's useful to take a look under the hood at how human brains are wired. You are probably familiar with phrases like "he broke my heart" and "the sting of rejection." You may have felt that another person's criticism felt like "a punch in the gut." One of the most interesting insights to emerge from the still relatively new field of social neuroscience is that our brain processes social pain—discomfort arising from our interactions with others—in much the same way as it processes the physical pain of a muscle cramp or a stubbed toe. There is more truth, in other words, to those figures of speech than you might ever have realized.

Studies by UCLA social neuroscientist Naomi Eisenberger have shown that the experience of both social and physical pain involves an area of the brain called the dorsal anterior cingulate cortex, or dACC, which has the highest density of opioid receptors—responsible for signaling pain and reward—of any region of the brain. Being rejected or treated unfairly activates the dACC just as a headache would. Eisenberger, along with her collaborator Nathan DeWall, was able to show that taking a thousand milligrams of Tylenol every day for three weeks resulted in the experience of significantly less *social* pain compared to a control group that took a placebo. Taking a painkiller had made the participants less sensitive to everyday rejection experiences. Evidently, you can treat your heartache and your hangover at the same time. (Why no one is marketing ibuprofen for this purpose yet, I can't imagine.)

But why would the human brain process a breakup like a broken arm? It's because pain—physical *and* social—is an important signal in our quest for survival. It alerts us that something is wrong, that we have injured either our bodies or our connections to others, both of which have been, throughout most of human history, literally essential for staying alive. As another UCLA social neuroscientist, Matt Lieberman (Eisenberger's husband and frequent collaborator), writes in his fascinating book *Social*, "Love and belonging might seem like a convenience we can live without, but our biology is built to thirst for connection because it is linked to our most basic survival needs."[5]

Human infants are born far more helpless and dependent than the offspring of other mammalian species. And adult humans, with all their cleverness, aren't exactly physically formidable creatures compared to our primate cousins. We have always needed to band together and cooperate with other humans to make it in the world; experiencing social pain is the brain's way of letting you know that you might be on the verge of getting tossed out of the band.

David Rock, director of the NeuroLeadership Institute, has spent years researching and writing about the specific types of social threat that can create a pain response—and all the unfortunate consequences that go with it, like diminished working memory and loss of focus—in our everyday interactions with others.[6] He integrated the research into five major categories.

Pain from Status *Threats*

Status refers to your value or sense of worth relative to others. It is a measure of your standing in a group—whether or not those around you respect you. Below our awareness, our brains are engaged in constant comparison, comparing ourselves to those with whom we work and socialize. (Research suggests that people frequently give themselves status rewards by engaging in what psychologists call *downward social comparison*—strategically comparing yourself to someone who is worse off, so you can feel better about you.) When you feel your friends or colleagues have disrespected, contradicted, or ignored you, it creates a strong status threat.

Pain from Certainty *Threats*

Human beings have a strong, innate desire for prediction. We want to know what is happening around us and, even more importantly, what's *going* to happen, so that we can be prepared to face it (or run away if we have to). Some of the greatest sources of stress people experience in their personal and professional lives revolve around interpersonal uncertainty of one kind or another, like the uncertainty of not knowing if your relationship with a romantic partner will last, or wondering if you will still have your job once your company merges with another.

Pain from Autonomy *Threats*

Along with the desire for prediction comes the desire for *control*. It's obviously not enough to know what's going to happen if you can't actually deal with it effectively. Psychologists have long argued that the need for *autonomy*—for a feeling of choice and the ability to take action in keeping with that choice—is one of the basic needs that characterize all human beings. When people feel out of control, they can not only experience momentary pain, but—if the feeling goes on long enough—endure periods of debilitating depression.

Pain from Relatedness *Threats*

Relatedness refers to your sense of belonging and connection with others, and it is arguably one of the most powerful sources of both reward and threat in the brain. Social psychologists have long studied our sensitivity to relatedness threats, like rejection. They have found that even objectively trivial instances of rejection can have profound effects.

Take, for example, the work of psychologist Kip Williams, who used a computer game he calls "Cyberball." Typically, in his studies, a participant will come into the lab and he will tell them that they are going to play a virtual ball-tossing game with two other online players.[7] Their only task is to "pass" the virtual ball to one another for a period of time. But the game is rigged—in the beginning, all three players pass the ball to one another, but soon, the two online players start passing the ball back and forth only to each other, leaving the participant completely excluded.

Who cares?, you are probably thinking. *It's just a stupid game in a psych experiment, right?* Wrong—participants in Williams's studies report significant drops in feelings of relatedness, positive mood, and even self-esteem. They are *very* unhappy about the other two online players rejecting them, even when it could not, practically speaking, matter less. Such is the power of a relatedness threat.

Pain from Fairness *Threats*

Human beings are remarkably sensitive to whether or not they are treated equitably, so much so that they will willingly accept outcomes that are less positive (or downright negative) in the interest of fairness. My personal favorite example of this need for fairness in action comes from a paradigm psychologists call the *ultimatum game*.

In the most common version of the game, people participate in pairs and are asked to split money between them. The researcher selects one person's name at random and makes them the money splitter, asking them to keep whatever amount of the total they choose and give the remainder to the partner. But the partner also has an important role to play—they can accept or reject the offer. If they reject the offer, *no one gets any money.*

From a purely rational perspective, even if the partner gets less than the money splitter, they should take it, because some money is generally better than none. But studies show that when the split is blatantly unequal (e.g., splitting $10, $9/$1 instead of $5/$5), the partner will almost always reject the offer, even though this means neither participant will get *any* money at all. When an outcome—even a positive one—seems unfair, the threat it produces can create surprising effects.

So now that you know about the five types of social threat, you have probably realized why asking for help is something we so often avoid. When you seek support from someone else, it opens up the possibility that you will experience all five kinds of social pain *at the same time*. By making a request of another person, many

people at least unconsciously feel that they have lowered their status and invited ridicule or scorn, particularly when the help request means revealing a lack of
knowledge or ability. Since you don't know how the person will answer, you've lowered your sense of certainty.
And since you have no choice but to accept their answer,
whatever it is, you've surrendered some of your autonomy as well. If they say no, it can feel like a personal
rejection, creating a relatedness threat. And, of course,
that "no" almost certainly won't feel very fair.

No wonder, then, that we avoid asking for help like
the plague. The plague might seem less dangerous in
comparison.

It Helps to Remember

- The idea of asking for even a small amount of help
  makes most of us horribly uncomfortable. Scientists
  have found that it can cause social pain that is every
  bit as real as physical pain.

- Asking for help is hard. Our fumbling, awkward, ret-
  icent ways of asking for help tend to backfire and
  make people less likely to actually help us. Our reluctance to ask for help means we often don't get the
  support or the resources we need.

- To get better at asking for help, we need to understand *reinforcements*—the small, subtle cues that motivate people to work with us. Once we do, we'll find an army of reinforcements—in the form of helpful people—riding to our rescue.

Chapter 2

We Assume Others Will Say No

The amount of agony we feel when asking for help depends, in part, on how likely people are to reject our request. And when it comes to figuring out that likelihood, well, frankly, we get it surprisingly wrong.

Vanessa Bohns doesn't tell her research participants to ask strangers for favors just for the fun of watching them squirm. She does it in order to try to understand a very perplexing phenomenon: people seriously underestimate how likely others are to comply with a direct request for help.

Before she sends them out on their help-seeking missions, Bohns asks participants to guess what percentage of the strangers they approach will agree to help (or in some versions, she asks them how many people they think they'll need to approach before one says yes). She then compares this estimate to the *actual* rates of help-ing. The differences are astounding.

In one of her studies with frequent collaborator Frank Flynn, Columbia University undergraduates were told to ask a stranger on campus for a favor—specifically, to complete a questionnaire that would take roughly five to ten minutes of their time.[1] The researchers asked the survey distributors to estimate how many people they would have to approach in order to get five completed surveys. They estimated twenty on average; the actual number was ten. The researchers repeated the experi-ment with two other requests: to briefly borrow a cell-phone, and to be escorted to the campus gym (only a short walk away). An identical pattern emerged both times.

In yet another study, the researchers had participants engage in a kind of scavenger hunt on campus, which required them to ask strangers trivia questions on an iPad and get points for each one answered correctly.[2] Participants not only underestimated the number of questions people would be willing to answer (twenty-five versus forty-nine), but also underestimated the effort they would put in, in terms of the number they would answer correctly (nineteen versus forty-six), and the total time they would spend on the task.

In yet another study, this one with real-world impact, researchers asked new volunteers who were raising

money for the Leukemia & Lymphoma Society to estimate the number of people they would need to contact
to reach their predetermined fund-raising goal, and the
average donation they would receive.[3] Volunteers estimated that they would need to contact 210 potential
donors, with an average donation of $48.33. In fact, they
had to contact only 122 potential donors, from whom
they received an average donation of $63.80.

In a recent review paper, Bohns described studies she
conducted with her colleagues in which participants
altogether asked more than fourteen thousand strangers
for various kinds of help.[4] She found that compliance—
the rate at which people will actually help—is underestimated on average by roughly 48 percent. In other
words, other people are roughly twice as likely to want
to be helpful as we think they are.

This is true even when requests for help are particularly large or irritating, or possibly illegal. In one study,
participants were told to go into the university library
and ask strangers to write the word "pickle," in pen, on
the page of a library book.[5] *Who would do that*, you wonder? Sixty-four percent of the people asked, that's who.
(The unfortunate participants who had to ask people
to vandalize the books had predicted only 28 percent
would agree to it.)

So, what's going on here? Why do those seeking
help seriously underestimate the likelihood of getting

help? Bohns and her colleagues argue that to a large extent, it's a failure of perspective taking. When a help seeker calculates the odds of getting help, they typically focus solely on how inconvenient or burdensome it will be for the person giving help. The more painful it is, the less likely they are to help. And that sounds logical enough, but that calculation is missing something very important. It's missing the cost to the potential helper of saying no.

Think back to the last time someone asked you for a favor, and you said no. How did it feel? Assuming you didn't hate the person in question, it probably felt pretty awful, didn't it? You were probably embarrassed; you might have experienced some shame or guilt. Your self-esteem might have even gone down a notch; after all, most of us care about being good, and good people are helpful, right?

There is, in short, a whole lot of psychological, inter-personal pressure on potential help givers to say yes. And this pressure to comply is very salient to the help giver, but much less so to the help seeker. Broadly speaking, most of us aren't very good at predicting other people's behavior, because we aren't natural perspective takers. Even though we have all been help givers, we fail to consider the perspective of *other* help givers when we most need to. As Bohns describes it, "We're so focused on our own emotional state and our own concerns that we can't get ourselves in the mindset of the people that we're asking."[6]

Help requests that are made face-to-face are the most successful, in no small part because the discomfort of saying no—the awkwardness and sense that you have violated social norms—increases exponentially. Indirect requests, like those made via email, do not cause discomfort to the same extent. However, help seekers do not usually take this into account and, when asked, prefer making indirect requests to direct ones.[7]

This underestimation-of-help effect exists everywhere, but is more pronounced in individualistic cultures like the United States and Western Europe compared to more collectivist, interdependent cultures like those in East Asia. In collectivist cultures, it seems, people are more keenly aware of the discomfort of saying no, so they calculate the odds of getting the help they seek a bit more accurately.

But it isn't simply a question of odds; research suggests that we also underestimate the amount of *effort* people will put in when they do agree to help us. Social norms don't just dictate that we help; we're supposed to do a good job helping, too. Ignoring this, help seekers don't expect people to go out of their way for them as much as they often do.

This is yet another reason why the motivation to ask for help isn't what it should be. Psychologists have long noted that our motivation to do anything can be (roughly) captured by the following model:

$$\text{Motivation} = \text{expectancy for success} \times \text{value of succeeding}$$

In other words, your motivation to do just about anything is a function of both (1) how likely you think you are to succeed at doing it, and (2) how much you will get out of it when you do.

In the case of asking for help, this theory suggests that being motivated to ask is a function of both the likelihood that the helper will say yes and the quality of the help you think you will receive. And we underestimate *both*.[8] Combine this double miscalculation with the five kinds of threat (discussed in chapter 1) that a request for support can cause, and it's no small wonder that most of us try to go it alone.

Bohns's favorite part of her experiments comes at the end, when her participants return to the lab after having spent an hour asking strangers for favors: "They bound back into the lab, all smiles, and surprised that it was such an easy task. And they leave thinking people are super-helpful, and that the world is a lovely place."[9]

When I deliberately think about it, I've had the same experience many times in my life. The time a stranger mailed me my wallet—with all the money still in it—after I had dropped it on a Manhattan sidewalk. The time I drove off the road into a snowy ditch, miles from anywhere that I could get a cellphone signal, and a group of men I'd never met before pulled over to the side of the road to help push my car out. The time a passerby found me while taking out the trash, cornered by a raccoon the size of a bear cub and chased it away. (Don't judge.) Every time, I remember feeling a warm glow inside, surprised but delighted that there was so much goodness in my fellow humans. The world did indeed seem like a lovely place.

People *want* to be helpful. Admittedly, not all people, but far more of us than you would imagine. And if you ask for the help you need, chances are good that you will get it, and then some. Steve Jobs certainly thought so. In 1994, a few years before he returned to Apple, one of the most successful men in recent history spoke to an interviewer about why it's so important to ask for what you need.

> Now, I've actually always found something to
> be very true, which is most people don't get
> those experiences because they never ask. I've
> never found anybody who didn't want to help
> me when I've asked them for help . . . I've never
> found anyone who's said no or hung up the
> phone when I called—I just asked. And when

people ask me, I try to be as responsive, to pay that debt of gratitude back. Most people never pick up the phone and call, most people never ask. And that's what separates, sometimes, the people that do things from the people that just dream about them.[10]

Underestimating the Helpfulness of People Who've Said No

There's one category of person we tend to underestimate even more than the normal run-of-the-mill person: anyone who has turned down our request in the past.

Earlier in this chapter, I said that turning down a request makes people really, really uncomfortable. It makes them feel as if they might be a bad person, because people are supposed to help one another. Well, now imagine how uncomfortable it is to turn down *two* requests.

It's relatively easy to find a justification for saying no once, which is why rates of helping aren't always 100 percent. *I'm terribly busy* or *I'm not feeling so well today* works once to assuage the guilt, but it doesn't usually work indefinitely. The second time a request is made, you need to have a really good reason to say no, or the pile of I'm-a-bad-person evidence starts to get too big to ignore. Which is why the research paints a very clear picture in this regard: people who have rejected an initial request for help are more likely to help the second time around, not less.

Take a look at the back of this book. See the quotes on the back? Those endorsements are what people in publishing call "blurbs." Authors and publishers send out early copies of books to influential people, hoping to secure a few kind words to the effect of "People should read this book because it's terrific," that can then be printed on the back cover or listed on the book's Amazon page.

I will freely admit that I hate asking for blurbs; I'm pretty sure all authors do. And I hate it for all the reasons that people hate asking for help more generally: it makes me feel embarrassed and vulnerable. But this particular book you are holding in your hands is my fifth, so I've been around the block a few times and can happily report that the asking gets easier.

With the first book, though, it was a bit of a nightmare for me. I literally pleaded with my agent not to make me do it. I was certain, just as Bohns would have predicted, that no one would agree to read the book, much less endorse it. But my agent insisted, and in the end (again, just as Bohns would have predicted), most of the people I asked did read it, and most said very nice things about it.

There was only one person who surprised me in a *negative* way—someone who I actually thought might read the book, because we have a close friend in common and knew one another a little. He ignored my request completely. I was annoyed at the time, but eventually forgot all about it, until it was time to try to get blurbs for my *second* book.

My agent once again sent me back out into the world to coax, cajole, and outright beg for endorsements. And he suggested I again approach the individual who had ignored me last time around. I thought he was crazy. *Why in the world would I ask that guy? If he didn't help me then, why would he help me now?* But, I got an amazing blurb, one that made me blush a little from the generosity of its praise. And looking back, I can think of many times when I've done something similar, when I've gone out of my way the second time around to make up for having been too selfish, lazy, or preoccupied to give someone the help they needed the first time.

I didn't know as much of the science on seeking help back then. So I didn't realize how wrong I was. For instance, Daniel Newark, Frank Flynn, and Vanessa Bohns conducted a study in which they told Stanford University students to ask fifteen strangers walking between two locations on campus to fill out a one-page questionnaire. Then, regardless of whether the stranger said yes or no to the first request, the participant had to follow it up with a second request—this time, to mail a letter.

Before heading out, the participants (no doubt, filled with dread) were asked to estimate the percentage of strangers who would say yes to the second request if they had said no to the first. They estimated only 18 percent would agree to mail the letter in that case, when actually 43 percent agreed to do so. Overall, requests for help were *higher* for the second request than the first. It seems no one likes to look like a jerk twice; once is bad enough.

A well-known sales tactic, called the "door-in-the-face" technique, is based on this very insight.[11] The idea of door-in-the-face is very simple: ask for something so difficult or outrageous that you know the other person is going to say no. Then follow it up with a much more reasonable request for whatever it is you actually wanted, and you are much more likely to get it.

In one of the most cited studies demonstrating how it works, a team lead by persuasion researcher Robert Cialdini asked participants if they would be willing to serve as a Big Brother or Big Sister to juvenile delinquents.[12] The request was a significant one, as it would entail a commitment of two hours a week for two years. Not surprisingly, every participant said no. The team then asked them if they would instead be willing to chaperone a one-day trip to the zoo for the same kids.

A control group of participants received only the second request without ever hearing the first, and 17 percent of them agreed to chaperone the zoo trip. But a whopping 50 percent of the ones who had first been asked—and said no—to serve as a Big Brother/Big Sister said yes to the zoo. In other words, the likelihood of saying yes to a smaller, second request after the first is rejected nearly *tripled*.

(In a great *Calvin and Hobbes* strip, Calvin tries to use the door-in-the-face technique to his advantage. In the first two panels, he asks his mother if he can set his bed mattress on fire or ride his tricycle off the roof. "No, Calvin," she replies each time. "Then can I have a cookie?" he asks. But she still says no. "She's on to me," he thinks. Which just goes to show that some subtlety in using this technique is probably helpful.)

Part of what may be happening when you use the door-in-the-face technique is something of a contrast effect: the second request seems so much smaller in comparison to the first that it no longer seems like a big deal. But the primary driver of its usefulness is clearly our sense of *social responsibility*—that we ought to be helpful and supportive when people ask us to be, and refusing two requests in a row made by the same person creates too much discomfort and guilt for us to bear.

This impulse to make up for our lapses in giving support is, broadly speaking, a good thing. It strengthens relationships and helps to mend ones that have become strained. When you approach someone for help who has rejected you in the past, you are not just more likely to get it; you are giving that person an opportunity to feel better about themselves, too. If you avoid seeking their help permanently, you won't be doing either of you any favors.

You may be wondering, what happens when you ask for a second favor from someone who actually *did* say yes to the first one? Are they less likely to help, having helped you once already? No! They are *also* more likely to help the second time around, thanks to the help seekers' friend, cognitive dissonance.

Cognitive dissonance is a strange and powerful psychological phenomenon. Human beings generally exhibit a reliable need for consistency; we prefer our beliefs to align with each another, and our actions to align with those beliefs. Holding inconsistent or contradictory views of something or someone (for instance, believing that John is a good person, while knowing at the same time that John cheats on his taxes) causes a kind of psychological pain called cognitive dissonance. People describe it, when you try to get them to put it into words, as a kind of nagging discomfort or a feeling that something is wrong. The only way to resolve the dissonance and get rid of the discomfort is to change one of the conflicting views (i.e., come up with a justification for why it's OK that John cheats on his taxes or decide that John is *not* actually a good person).

Helping you in the past and refusing to help you now would create an inconsistency, or contradiction, that would bring on the uncomfortable tension of cognitive dissonance. Research suggests that people will be willing to help in increasingly effortful and inconvenient ways after granting an initial request. This, too, has inspired a sales tactic that is more or less the reverse of door-in-the-face, called the foot-in-the-door technique.

To use the foot-in-the-door technique, simply ask for something relatively small or effortless that you know the other person will say yes to; once you have secured that yes, follow it up with a second, larger request. (A friend once used this on me to great success. First she asked me if she could drop off a plant at my apartment so I could water it while she was away for two weeks. I enthusiastically said, "Yes, of course!" She then followed it with a request to drop off her St. Bernard as well. I said yes and then spent almost a year finding dog hair.)

It's somewhat astonishing that our intuitions about whether and when other people will be willing to help us, and how they will feel about us when they do, are so terribly wrong. After all, we are all help *givers* as well as help *seekers*. We know how difficult it is to say no. We know that we don't like people less simply because they've asked for our help. If only we could keep all that in mind when it's our turn to need support, the asking would be a whole lot easier.

It Helps to Remember

- Help seekers consistently underestimate their chances of getting the help they've asked for. This is great news! People are actually much more likely to help us than we assume.

- For lots of us, it is really, really painful to say no. In fact, if we have said no once already, we're less likely to say no a second time. It's just too hard.

- We are less likely to say no when we've already said yes, because of cognitive dissonance. "I am a nice, helpful person," we think to ourselves, and we want to keep thinking of ourselves that way.

- This is all very good news for the help seekers out there.

Chapter 3

We Assume Asking for Help Makes Us Less Likable

Founding Father Benjamin Franklin was, among other things, a very observant fellow. Some of his observations led to remarkable inventions, like the lightning rod, bifocals, the Franklin stove, the catheter, and swim fins. (Yes, swim fins. Really. You can look it up.) He was also a keen observer of his fellow man, identifying and extolling what he believed to be the thirteen core character virtues that would lead, once mastered, to "moral perfection," including *temperance, order, frugality,* and *moderation.* (He recorded his successes and failures at mastering each virtue in a daily journal and noted that he was "surprised to find myself so much fuller of faults than I had imagined." You and me both, Ben.)

Another of his more useful observations concerned the question of help seeking—namely, whether one might suffer a loss of standing in the eyes of the person from whom one seeks a favor. In his autobiography, he told the following story:

> My first promotion was my being chosen, in 1736, clerk of the General Assembly. The choice was made that year without opposition; but the year following, when I was again proposed (the choice, like that of the members, being annual), a new member made a long speech against me, in order to favor some other candidate. I was, however, chosen, which was the more agreeable to me, as, besides the pay for the immediate service as clerk, the place gave me a better opportunity of keeping up an interest among the members, which secured to me the business of printing the votes, laws, paper money, and other occasional jobs for the public, that, on the whole, were very profitable. I therefore did not like the opposition of this new member, who was a gentleman of fortune and education, with talents that were likely to give him, in time, great influence in the House, which, indeed, afterwards happened.
> I did not, however, aim at gaining his favor by paying any servile respect to him, but, after some

time, took this other method. Having heard that he had in his library a certain very scarce and curious book, I wrote a note to him, expressing my desire of perusing that book, and requesting he would do me the favor of lending it to me for a few days. He sent it immediately, and I returned it in about a week with another note, expressing strongly my sense of the favor. When we next met in the House, he spoke to me (which he had never done before), and with great civility; and he ever after manifested a readiness to serve me on all occasions, so that we become great friends, and our friendship continued to his death. This is another instance of the truth of an old maxim I had learned, which says, **"He that has once done you a kindness will be more ready to do you another than he whom you yourself have obliged."** [Emphasis added.][1]

On the surface, this story doesn't make any sense. A man who cared so little for Franklin that he never bothered to speak to him—who even lobbied for him to lose his position as clerk—proceeded to loan him a rare and valuable book and then *liked Franklin more for having done so.* But it actually makes a great deal of sense, once you remember *cognitive dissonance* (from chapter 2).

Without a doubt, Franklin's book borrowing would have created some serious cognitive dissonance for the book owner. As Bohns's work shows, the book owner would have felt significant pressure to comply with Franklin's request. But then having done so, he would be left with two contradictory thoughts rattling around in his mind: (1) I just loaned a rare and valuable book to Ben Franklin, and (2) I really don't like Ben Franklin.

Since the book owner could not travel back in time and refuse to loan him the book, the only remaining way to get rid of the dissonance was to decide that, in point of fact, *he did indeed like Ben Franklin.* Shifting to a positive view of Franklin solves the problem entirely; after all, doing a favor for someone you like is a perfectly natural and consistent thing to do. In this way, cognitive dissonance provides help givers with a powerful motivation to hold their help recipients in high regard. When they do, there is no tension, and the engine of the mind keeps running smoothly.

Most people—very wrongly—assume that giving help makes a far better impression than asking for help. In fact, people can have mixed feelings about receiving help, sometimes even resenting the helper out of a combination of embarrassment and self-blame. (*I hate that I couldn't do this without help . . . and now you're making me look bad. Great.*) Helpers, on the other hand, are remarkably consistent. They tend to like the people whom they help *more*, not less, after helping them.

In the 1960s, psychologists Jon Jecker and David Landy conducted perhaps my favorite study illustrating this phenomenon.[2] The experimenter, "Mr. Boyd," greeted college students who came to the lab and told them that they would be answering questions and would receive money for every correct answer. Mr. Boyd was— very deliberately—not the nicest person. He spoke in a cold monotone, refrained from doing anything even remotely friendly, and said things like, "Pay attention because I don't want to have to repeat myself."

After answering the questions (which were rigged so that students got them all correct), one of three things happened:

- One-third of the group was given their money and then asked to fill out a questionnaire, which included the question, "How much do you like Mr. Boyd personally?" This was the control group.

- One-third of the group was given their money and then stopped by a secretary who explained that the psychology department actually needed the money back. Almost all of these participants agreed to give back the money. They then completed the questionnaire.

- The final third was given their money and
  then was approached by Mr. Boyd himself
  with a request: "I was wondering if you would
  do me a favor. The funds for this experiment
  have run out and I am using my own money
  to finish the experiment. As a favor to me,
  would you mind returning the money you
  won?" Again, almost all participants agreed
  and then completed the questionnaire.

So, what did everyone think of Mr. Boyd? On a
12-point scale, the control group—the ones who got to
keep their money—gave Mr. Boyd an average liking
score of 4.8. Those who had to give their money back for
the benefit of the psychology department liked him even
less, rating him a 4.0. But those whom Mr. Boyd had
asked for a favor—the ones who gave their money back
to benefit him directly—rated him a 7.6. Other versions
of the same study showed that the size of this effect
depends directly on the magnitude of the money won;
the more money participants gave back to Mr. Boyd, the
more they liked him.

In other words, doing a favor for a jerk makes him
seem like less of a jerk, and doing a *big* favor for a jerk
makes him start to seem like a great guy. Thanks to cognitive dissonance, the more you give him, the better he
must be. Otherwise, something is terribly wrong.

So there is very little reason to fear that asking for help will make someone like you less. You might want to think seriously about saying yes when people offer you favors, praise, support, or gifts, even when you don't really need them or your pride tells you otherwise. They'll like you more for it.

We Underestimate How Good Giving Makes People Feel

A small group of people are chronic givers—about 20 percent of the population, according to Wharton professor Adam Grant, who has been studying them scientifically for many years. Givers help other people frequently and generously, without seeming to stop and think much about what might be in it for them. If anything, they seem to *prefer* to give more than they get. They are distinguished in Grant's work from *matchers*, who are fairness-driven and give more or less in keeping with what they get from others, and *takers* who, as the name implies, are pretty much jerks.

Givers are consistently the most *and* least successful people in any industry—everyone from software engineers to venture capitalists to salespeople who work at LensCrafters. When they are the least successful, it tends to be because of the burnout that can accompany helping others too much and not spending enough time on their own goals. But those givers who are able to strike a balance benefit enormously, it seems, from their own giving natures. They have the richest, deepest network of connections and supporters, exert a profound influence on those around them, and like a rising tide, seem to win not by defeating others but by creating situations that lift everyone's boat. They live enriched, fulfilling lives dripping with meaning and purpose.

I am not a giver. I reacted to half of Grant's stories of extraordinary givers with some version of, "Wait, she did *what?*" No matter how hard I tried, I couldn't manage to convince myself that I was one of these amazing and inspiring people. I didn't fit the bill.

But since about 80 percent of the population aren't givers, I am in, well, if not good then at least abundant company. Not that we *never* give, of course. For the rest of us in the other 80 percent, it's more accurate to say that we give sometimes, and then sometimes we don't. But even for us semi-selfish people, we're a lot happier when we give than when we don't. And that's something that people reluctant to ask for our help almost always forget. Let's take a closer look at how, specifically, giving makes givers feel good.

Helping Boosts Your Mood

One of the most reliable benefits of offering someone else support is how it lifts your spirits. Psychologists speak of the "warm glow" that prosocial behaviors confer.[3] You can see it in the faces of people distributing food in soup kitchens, walking the dogs in animal shelters, and mentoring at-risk youth in inner cities. But helping needn't be quite so lofty as all that, either. I have felt a touch of the warm glow when doing something as mundane (and relatively effortless) as holding a door open for a mom with an unwieldy stroller, or pointing out that a stranger had dropped his glove a few steps back.

Even playing a simple word game can boost your mood, if you think someone might actually benefit from you playing it. Researchers Frank Martela and Richard Ryan asked undergraduates to play a game in which they were to identify the correct synonym for a word from a set of four alternatives.[4] (Admittedly, this sounds like a terribly boring game.) Half were then told that for every correct answer, a rice donation would be made to the UN World Food Programme. The experimenter pointed out that "by playing the game, you can make a real-life contribution to world poverty and society at large."

In case you are curious, the donation was ten grains of rice per correct answer. And yes, that is a fairly pathetic-sounding amount of rice, which frankly makes the results of the study that much more remarkable. Despite the fact that there were no differences in how well players actually played across conditions—and despite the relatively tiny amounts of actual rice involved—players whose efforts could help others experienced significant increases in positive mood, vitality, and well-being.

(By the way, this game is perfectly real, and you can play it, too. Just go to www.Freerice.com. Since it began in October, 2007, FreeRice has donated over 95 billion grains of rice to feed the hungry, a not-at-all pathetic amount of rice that has helped the World Food Programme successfully feed millions of people in need.)

Helping Makes Things Less Awful

Sometimes we decide to help others in order to put a bit of a spring in our step. But people are often particularly likely to want to help—and to reap the mood benefits of helping—not so much to achieve a great mood, but in order to repair a *bad* one. Robert Cialdini (of *door-in-the-face* and *foot-in-the-door* technique fame) has long argued that *negative state relief* is a primary driver of altruistic action. One oft-cited story of US President Abraham Lincoln nicely illustrates this:

> An amusing incident occurred in connection with one of these journeys [on the judicial circuit in Illinois], which gives a pleasant glimpse into the good lawyer's heart. He was riding by a deep slough, in which, to his exceeding pain, he saw a pig struggling, and with such faint efforts that it was evident that he could not extricate himself from the mud. Mr. Lincoln looked at the pig and the mud which enveloped him, and then looked at some new clothes with which he had but a short time before enveloped himself. Deciding against the claims of the pig, he rode on, but he could not get rid of the vision of the poor brute, and, at last, after riding two miles, he turned back, determined to rescue the animal at the expense of his new clothes.
>
> Arrived at the spot, he tied his horse, and coolly went to work to build of old rails a passage to the bottom of the hole. Descending on these rails, he seized the pig and dragged him out, but not without serious damage to the clothes he wore. Washing his hands in the nearest brook, and wiping them on the grass, he mounted his gig and rode along. He then fell to examining the motive that

sent him back to the release of the pig. At the first thought, it seemed to be pure benevolence, but, at length, he came to the conclusion that it was self-ishness, for he certainly went to the pig's relief in order (as he said to the friend to whom he related the incident) to "take a pain out of his mind."[5]

The relief of suffering is, of course, a powerful motivator of helping, but more often than we realize, it is our *own* suffering that we are equally preoccupied by. In their studies, Cialdini and his colleagues show, for instance, that people whose moods were negatively affected by witnessing an innocent individual being harmed were more likely to be helpful to a third party than those in a neutral mood, unless they had *already* had their spirits lifted by receiving a surprise gift. With their distress gone, they were no more likely to be helpful than anyone else.[6]

Of course, no one is suggesting that people literally think to themselves, "I'm awfully cranky. I'd better go make a donation to the Red Cross." But on an unconscious level, we intuitively know that lending a hand can do wonders for how we feel. More than that, studies suggest that we may not bother with being helpful when we think it *can't* improve our mood.

Cialdini and colleagues Gloria Manuncia and Donald Baumann cleverly illustrated this in a study in which participants entered the lab and the researchers told them they would be taking a (perfectly safe) fast-acting memory drug called Mnemoxine. They told half of the participants that Mnemoxine had a strange side effect; it would chemically preserve whatever mood they were in when they took it for roughly thirty minutes. So if they were happy around the time they took the pill, they'd be happy, no matter what happened, for the next half hour.

Participants' moods were altered when researchers asked them, immediately after taking the (placebo) pill, to reflect on either a very sad or a happy memory. Finally, about five to ten minutes later, upon "leaving" the study, an experimenter posing as a blood drive volunteer asked participants if they might be willing to help the cause by making anywhere from one to ten phone calls to regular donors on behalf of the drive.

Consistent with the idea that helping can be a way to lift mood, people who had been forced to relive sad memories were more helpful (i.e., made more phone calls) than those who had been given a happier walk down memory lane, but only when they believed getting into a better mood was *possible*. Sad participants who thought they were stuck with sadness for another twenty to twenty-five minutes actually helped significantly less than those stuck in happy mode.

Which explains why deeply clinically depressed people aren't necessarily running around gathering donations for UNICEF door-to-door to cure what ails them. Depression, as opposed to just sadness, is characterized by a sense of permanence—the (largely inaccurate) belief that how you feel right now is never going to change. When people believe that a boost in mood isn't even possible, they tend not to seek one.

Incidentally, helping doesn't just provide an antidote to sadness. It's also a great way to rid ourselves of guilt. Psychologists argue that guilt—a state often characterized by tension, remorse, and anxiety—serves the function of helping to preserve and strengthen social bonds. It reminds us to honor our commitments, shoulder our responsibilities, and call our mothers regularly. When we do something harmful to someone else, guilt motivates us to repair the damage, so that we don't get booted out of the tribe. Knowing that we will feel guilty often keeps us from doing bad things in the first place.[7] But when we do end up feeling guilt for whatever reason, there are few more effective ways of convincing ourselves that we aren't completely despicable than lending someone a hand.

More Helping = Greater Life Satisfaction

You won't be surprised to learn that the more you give, the more rewarding and fulfilling your life will be. (The famous Christmas classic *It's a Wonderful Life* is an exercise in exactly this premise. It is literally in the title.) Studies show, for instance, that people who belong to charity organizations or engage in volunteer work have higher levels of life satisfaction, physical health, and self-esteem. They actually feel better, look better, and like themselves more.[8] But once again, giving need not be quite so grand to provide such benefits. Simple things like giving directions to a stranger or letting someone else go ahead in line can lead to increases in well-being. And if you really want to improve your quality of life, try spending money on other people.[9]

As the saying goes, money doesn't buy happiness. Increases in wealth have been shown to have a very modest effect on well-being, once people have enough money to ensure their basic needs are met. Psychologist Elizabeth Dunn has argued, however, that this is primarily because people don't spend their money on the right things. Money that is well spent can indeed increase well-being, but here, "spent well" is synonymous with "spent on someone other than you."

For instance, Dunn and her colleagues Lara Aknin and Michael Norton asked a nationally representative sample of over six hundred Americans to indicate their monthly income, their happiness level, and how much they spent each month on themselves (in bills, expenses, and gifts for themselves) versus others (in gifts for others and donations to charity). Personal spending was completely unrelated to happiness, but prosocial spending—spending on others—predicted reliably greater happiness.

In a second study, Dunn and colleagues followed sixteen employees who had received a profit-sharing bonus from their company. Once again, employees who spent more of their bonus on others experienced greater subsequent happiness over the next six to eight weeks. And, importantly, the way they spent the money was a stronger predictor of happiness than the amount of the bonus itself.

In a final study, they gave participants either $5 or $20 and instructed them to either buy themselves a gift or spend it on a gift for someone else or a charitable donation. Once again, those who spent the money on others experienced the most happiness. And again, the amount of money had no effect in either condition.

So, why am I telling you all this? It's not actually to try to get you to be more of a giver, though it's pretty clear from the research that if you and I both upped the amount of help and support we gave to others, we'd be better off. What I *am* trying to do, however, is to get you comfortable with the idea of *asking* for help. In the previous two chapters, you learned that people are more likely to help than we think they are, that they give you better-quality help than we think they will, and that they will like you more—not less—for having helped you. Now you know that giving them the opportunity to help you can provide them with real, lasting benefits. We could even make the argument that *not* asking for help is a selfish thing, in that it robs other people of one of life's most reliable boosts to well-being.

Now that you know what's in it for them, let's turn to the next challenge: giving *them* what they need from *you* to make help possible.

It Helps to Remember

- Receiving help often fills us with mixed feelings. And we consequently assume that asking for help will make us seem less likable or less competent. But research shows that helpers like the people they've helped *more* after helping them.

- Helping confers a host of other benefits on the helper. It boosts our moods, fills us with a rosy glow, and generally makes the world a little less horrible.

- We should feel a little less uncomfortable when we have to ask for help. Though it might fill us with dread to have to ask, asking the right way actually opens up an opportunity for other people to feel really, really good about themselves and about us.

Part Two

How to Ask
Anyway

Chapter 4

The Inherent Paradox in Asking for Help

About a year ago, I was helping a friend from graduate school put together a particularly complicated and intimidating IKEA bookshelf. Ever since I had proven myself decent at this sort of thing years ago, I'd been her go-to gal for furniture assembly. (Honestly, it's not that I'm particularly handy; I'm just weirdly good at understanding poorly illustrated instructions.)

Assembling bookshelves is probably pretty low on most people's list of "ways I enjoy helping my friends"— right below *water my plants while I'm away*, but still above *help me move into my new apartment*—and I'm no different. Yet, I eagerly agreed to her request when she phoned me, and even found myself looking forward to lending a hand on the drive over.

Many hours (and many bruises from mishandling shelves and dropping a power tool on my foot) later, we stood shoulder to shoulder, gazing proudly upon the wonder of a fully constructed SPROINK or VERBLANGT or whichever shelving system it was. My friend turned to me at this point and said, "Heidi, thank you. You are always so helpful and generous." She meant it.

But nice as it was to hear, this statement struck me immediately as somehow *wrong*.

You see, I'm not *always* so helpful and generous. Far from it. That very morning, in fact, I had made a whole series of unhelpful and entirely selfish decisions.

First, I had turned down a request to review a submission to a scientific journal because the topic seemed boring and I didn't want to spend the time on it, even though I know reviewing papers is a necessary part of the business of science, and despite the fact that it would probably have taken the same amount of time as the shelf assembly and been far less physically painful.

Then I chose to strategically ignore an email asking parents to volunteer to help with an after-school ice cream party for my daughter's fourth-grade class. Because, I told myself, I had done it the year before so I should be off the hook now for several years. Plus, feeding fourth graders ice cream is a job that is both thankless and sticky.

Finally, I'd grudgingly agreed to do the laundry. I realize laundry is a mundane part of everyday adult life.

However, I hate laundry about as much as it is possible for an adult human being to hate a perfectly mundane task. So I'd done it, but only after emitting a long and loud sigh, rolling my eyes so hard I'm surprised I didn't sprain something, and muttering, "Fine, I'll do it. But I'm not folding it."

Having spent the first section of this book explaining why we really shouldn't be so hesitant about asking for help, even if it does feel a bit awkward, I'm now going to do a bit of an about-face: the truth is, asking for help can be a bit tricky. If it wasn't, you wouldn't be reading this book. As we'll see in this chapter, although most people do have an innate desire to feel helpful, they really hate feeling *compelled* to help. But how can you ask someone to help without, in some sense, compelling them?

The Four Possible Responses to a Request for Help

I'll wager that just about every morning, you send out emails asking for some form of professional favor, maybe advice on a project, or help tracking down a difficult-to-find resource, or an introduction and recommendation to a colleague. Once recipients have read your request, they are going to have one of the same four reactions, more or less.

Reaction 1: No

An explicit "No, I'm sorry I can't help with that," like my response to the academic journal, is the answer most of us are usually expecting to hear. However, as discussed in chapter 2, it's actually a fairly rare response. It's pretty hard to give a clean and untroubled no when someone asks you to do something. Bartleby the Scrivener might have been able to say, "I would prefer not to," with ease, but the rest of us seem to struggle with it. While it's statistically unlikely your response will be met with a clear no, it is possible.

Reaction 2: Silence

The more popular alternative seems to be to simply ignore the request until it sinks down deep enough in their inbox that recipients can pretend to themselves that they forgot to answer or never saw it in the first place, as I did with the email from my daughter's school. (And I am appalled by how often I go with this option.) The benefit of reaction 2 is that recipients don't experience the discomfort of saying no. The downside, of course, is that they leave you, the sender, hanging, which is almost certainly more annoying and anxiety producing. And the upshot is the same: they don't help you.

Either reaction 1 or 2 will probably cause the recipient to feel at least a little uncomfortable, if not experience a full-blown bout of *I-am-a-terrible-person.*

Reaction 3: Grudging Yes

"Ugh. OK, I guess I have to . . . eventually" is a very popular reaction, particularly when there is really no avoiding you, the person making the request. By choosing reaction 3, the recipients of your request are able to avoid the guilt of *not* helping, while minimizing inconvenience to themselves and putting out as little effort as possible. Of course, the downside is that they will derive no pleasure or self-affirmation at all from helping. At best, they will feel some small relief when they can cross the favor off their to-do list.

Reaction 4: Enthusiastic Yes

"YES!" is hands-down the best reaction for all parties involved. We all know what it's like to be genuinely delighted to be able to help someone, to feel eager and energized by the prospect of providing that help, and to willingly go above and beyond—sometimes spontaneously offering up other, even more effective ways in which we might be helpful. *You'd like me to introduce you to John? Gladly! While I'm at it, would you like an introduction to Susan and Alex, too? And is anyone watering your plants while you're away?*

When people have reaction 4, they not only give their very best, but they *feel* their very best. They experience surges of happiness and well-being that have been well documented by decades of research. They like themselves more. And, of course, they strengthen their relationships with those to whom they give their help.

But an enthusiastic yes is actually fairly rare. If it's so great, why don't people have this reaction all the time?

Some psychologists focus on what they call *individual differences* as the primary way of explaining different behaviors. Some people have this kind of personality, so they do X, and others have this other kind of personality, so they do Y. Adam Grant's analysis of givers and takers (mentioned in the previous chapter) would fall into this category. Chronic givers like helping (or dislike the pain of not helping) so much that they give enthusiastic yeses almost all the time, even sometimes to the point of shortchanging their own goals, desires, and needs. But they're only 20 percent of the population.

And (as you may have noticed) human beings aren't always consistent and predictable. Most of us do give *sometimes*. And not other times. So what's different about the times we choose to give and the times we choose not to?

Social psychologists like myself tend to want to explain behavior less in terms of personality (though obviously that's still important) and more in terms of the context or situational forces at play. *When* are people helpful and generous, as opposed to just minimally helpful or completely unhelpful? *What* motivates each of those reactions, and what kinds of rewards or incentives does a person need to elicit the most helpful, supportive behavior, not just once, but again and again?

Understanding the answers to these questions is really, really important if you want to get anywhere in this world. No one succeeds alone. Yes, everyone has certain job responsibilities or "have to's," so being totally uncooperative is often not an option. But people do absolutely have options when it comes to how they prioritize the work they do each day, and how much of their best effort they put into it. Your coworkers may have to help you—they may owe you a grudging yes—but they don't have to be eager to help you. Whether or not you get an enthusiastic yes is the question, and the surprising answer is that it's more under your control than you may realize.

The IKEA bookshelf story contains examples of many of the key elements that I'll be returning to again and again in this part of the book. *I am weirdly good at doing that sort of task. The help seeker was an old friend from an important time in my life. She expressed gratitude in a particular way. I was able to stand with her and see the results of my efforts.* Each of these elements provided a type of reinforcement I needed to motivate the highest-quality help I had to offer—reinforcements that were missing from the other requests for help I received that same morning.

Having to Help versus Wanting to Help

Psychologists who study prosocial behavior have long realized that there is more than one thing going on when one person helps another—more than one potential source of motivation. Of course, true to our long-standing tradition, most of us in the field can't quite agree on what those sources of motivation are or what to call them. Roughly speaking though, the distinctions researchers have made map onto one another well and can be boiled down to this: Are you helping because you *have* to or because you *want* to?

I Did It My Way

Human beings have psychological needs. That much is clear. How many needs, and exactly what they are, is still a matter of some debate (seriously, we argue about everything), but most psychologists agree that among these critical needs is the need for *autonomy*. (You may recall, in chapter 1, that autonomy is one of the five categories of social threat that activate a pain center in our brains. When we feel a lack of autonomy, it hurts.)

Autonomy is about choice and control. Specifically, it's about choosing your own goals, activities, and experiences. It's about feeling as if what you do is an authentic reflection of *who you are*—your own values and preferences. In the United States, we have expressions we frequently use to capture this notion, like being *captain of your own ship* and *charting your own course*. Or, if you prefer the more modern, less nautical version, *you do you*.

When we engage in a behavior because we choose to, not because we have to, we are what psychologists call *intrinsically motivated*. And without exaggeration, research has clearly shown over the last thirty or forty years that this type of motivation is just the best. When you are intrinsically motivated, you find greater interest and enjoyment in what you do, even when it's challenging. You are more creative in your thinking, and you absorb more new knowledge. You are better at hanging in there even when the going gets tough. Across the board, intrinsic motivation leads to greater improvement, superior performance, and a deeper sense of satisfaction.

For example, middle schoolers who feel as if their gym teachers give them "choices and options" report liking exercise more and get more exercise in their free time.[1]

People in weight-loss programs that offer the feeling of choice lose more weight.[2] (Similar results have been shown in programs for diabetes management, smoking cessation, alcohol treatment, and methadone maintenance.[3]) Students with autonomy-supportive teachers get better grades, are more creative and challenge seeking, and are more likely to stay in school.[4] People who adhere to particular religious practices because they want to have greater well-being and life satisfaction, while those who go to a church and follow its teachings from a sense of obligation do not.[5] Nursing home residents who can choose from a set of activities each day and can arrange their rooms according to their own liking live longer.[6]

I'm not finished. Intrinsic motivation is so magical that it can apparently do something psychologists once thought impossible. Imagine if there were something you could add to your car's engine, so that after driving it a hundred miles, you'd end up with *more* gas in the tank than you started with. That would be great, right? Well, intrinsic motivation does something similar for your own personal gas tank: it can make you feel energized—rather than exhausted—by mentally taxing work.

In a fascinating set of studies, psychologists at Colorado State University gave participants a task that was particularly draining and then varied whether the next task was difficult but personally interesting, or relatively easy but nothing anyone would ever *want* to do.

They found that people who worked on the personally interesting task put in more effort and performed much better (despite being tired) than those who worked on the have-to task, even though it was actually *harder* than the have-to task. In other words, experiencing intrinsic motivation restored their energy and gave them a tangible advantage.[7]

In another study, the researchers found that experiencing intrinsic motivation resulted in better performance on a *subsequent* task as well. In other words, you don't just do a better job on task A because you find task A inherently interesting; you do a better job on follow-up task B *because you found task A inherently interesting.* The replenished energy flows into whatever you do next.

(Incidentally, each of these studies compared the effects of intrinsic motivation and good mood, and found that while people do get some replenishment of energy from being happy, they get much more from being interested in and engaged by what they do.)

I Did It Your Way

Feeling controlled, on the other hand, results in a far less effective and satisfying state of affairs. It destroys any intrinsic motivation you might have had and replaces it with the feeling that you might as well just get this over with. No one likes feeling micromanaged, obviously, but what *is* surprising is how even subtle forms of control can have such a strong (and negative) impact.

One of my favorite examples of the effect of feeling controlled comes from a study by intrinsic motivation researcher Mark Lepper.[8] He and his colleagues began by studying one of the most intrinsically motivated things you can think of: preschoolers playing with magic markers. Obviously, you don't need to tell four-year-olds to play with magic markers. You don't need to threaten them with punishments or entice them with rewards. They just do it, because they *want* to. But what happens to their natural desire when you try to control it?

Lepper told some of the children he was observing that they could earn a special "Good Player Award" for drawing pictures with the magic markers, and they did so with enthusiasm, using the markers longer than the children who weren't offered the award. That's great, right? The award was motivating! Except actually, it wasn't. Once Lepper gave the award and offered no new prizes, the children stopped wanting to play with the markers altogether. Their intrinsic motivation to play with the markers was completely destroyed by the reward. For them, markers became something they only played with when they got something in return. But for the kids who never got an award, markers were still something they played with because they wanted to.

Rewards aren't the only things that can make us feel controlled. Threats, surveillance, deadlines, and other pressures have the same effect, because they make us feel as if we are no longer free to act as we wish. Which brings us to the issue at hand: What happens to the likelihood and quality of helping, when people feel as if they *have* to help you? What does controlled helping look like?

It's not good.

How We Inadvertently Make People Feel Compelled to Help

Why do people sometimes feel controlled when they are asked for help? For starters, as Vanessa Bohns's research described in chapter 2 shows, people experience significant psychological discomfort when turning down a request for help. *Good people are helpful*, we think to ourselves on some level, so if we choose not to help, where does that leave us? Also, rejecting another person in need creates an awkward tension that isn't easily resolved, even when we offer apologies and justifications for the rejection. Really, slinking away quickly is your only option.

Moreover, when someone asks you for help and you even consider saying no, you *know* that discomfort is coming. It's like a form of punishment. And generally speaking, when you know that a course of action will lead to punishment, and your only way of avoiding it is to give in to the request, you feel controlled.

That's the catch-22 of asking for help: if people say yes, they might feel controlled. If they say no, they might feel like real jerks. There is clearly no winning here. And there are circumstances that make the feeling of having to help even more acute.

Can You Do Me a Favor?

Imagine that you are walking through New York City's Penn Station—one of the city's busiest commuter hubs—on your way to work. A college student approaches you with a clipboard in her hand. (If you knew at this point that the student was from Bohns's research lab, I'm assuming you would use the good sense God gave you and run.)

The student asks, "Excuse me, would you fill out a questionnaire?" How do you think you would respond?

Now, what if the student asked instead, "Can you do me a favor?" And then waited until you responded (with something like "Yeah, sure, what is it?" as most people do) before asking, "Would you fill out a questionnaire?" Do you think you might respond differently?

I'm guessing right now you are thinking that there is no real difference between these two approaches, so you'd respond the same way in both cases, and you'd say no. But I'm here to tell you that you are wrong. The second version—the one that asked for and obtained commitment to a *favor* before revealing the request—yielded an 84 percent cooperation rate, compared to only 57 percent for the non-favor version (which is actually still impressive. People really are helpful).[9]

According to Bohns and her research coauthor Frank Flynn, asking someone to essentially precommit to a favor induces higher levels of helping. It basically ramps up the potential discomfort of saying no. After all, not only are good people helpful, but *you just said you would do this person a favor.* Now you are a person who goes back on their word, too. Nice going.

Right now, you might be thinking to yourself, "Hey, that sounds like a great way to get people to help me when I need them to! I'll get them to precommit." But be warned, this approach has a significant potential downside for you. After filling out their questionnaires, the researchers asked the New York City commuters how large a monetary gift they should receive for the trouble they went to. The people who had precommitted to a favor asked for more than *twice* as much money. They resented having been made to feel trapped and wanted to be compensated for their pain and suffering accordingly.

In other words, influence tactics can have trade-offs. In the short term, you may get what you want. But in the long term, there is now someone in your life who feels as if you owe them, big time. Which, ironically, may leave *you* feeling controlled.

You Owe Me

Reciprocity is a powerful force in human psychology. Just think of all the expressions we use in our daily lives that capture the belief that we should give what we get, and get what we give:

> An eye for an eye.
>
> Do unto others as you would have them do unto you (or The Golden Rule).
>
> Turnabout is fair play.
>
> You reap what you sow.

One of the most pervasive norms (i.e., rules of behaving that a group or society explicitly or implicitly adheres to) across all cultures is the norm of reciprocity. People are expected (and expect of themselves) to give what they receive in kind. And generally, they do.

This is driven by two influences. When someone does you a good turn, most people experience both a feeling of gratitude and sense of obligation or debt. You might assume that it's the latter that leads to greater helping, but gratitude itself can also increase helping, even toward those who haven't done a damn thing for you. Studies show, for example, that when people are made to feel grateful, they are not only more likely to help their benefactor, they are more likely to help perfect strangers in need of assistance. (But that effect disappears after about thirty minutes. People tend to not *stay* grateful, as I'm sure you've noticed.)[10]

There are actually three flavors of reciprocity, according to research by Frank Flynn.[11] *Personal reciprocity* is a kind of negotiated exchange, or barter. It's *you scratch my back, and I'll scratch yours.* For example, when coworkers decide to exchange work shifts, or roommates take turns doing the dishes, that's personal reciprocity. It doesn't usually lead to helping beyond what was explicitly negotiated; it doesn't really produce gratitude, and the sense of obligation you might feel is satisfied by the terms of the exchange. In essence, personal reciprocity is strictly business.

Relational reciprocity is exactly what it sounds like: the kind of reciprocity we engage in in our actual relationships (with friends, romantic partners, family members, etc.). It isn't an explicit deal. You just tend to be helpful to one another, assuming that in the future the relationship partner will support you when needed. There is no keeping score. (Unless, of course, one person repeatedly fails to provide support in return. That usually gets noticed. And it doesn't end well.) Relational reciprocity creates both gratitude and a sense of obligation, but that sense of obligation is specific to the relationship partner only.

Collective reciprocity is a kind of generalized exchange of helping, at the level of a group. It's when you lend a hand because you share an identity with someone. This identity could be something quite broad, like helping someone of the same race, nationality, or religion, or something very specific, like helping someone who is a fellow member of your department or your local PTA, or who plays in your bowling league.

Collective helping, like relational helping, occurs without concern for immediate return on your helping investment. You don't expect help from that specific person in return, necessarily, but have a broader (often implicit) faith that helping someone who is similar to you in some way is good for you, because you can expect help from similar others in return when you need it.

Moreover, there is still that element of feeling just a little controlled in both relational and collective responsibility—the feeling that I *ought* to help my friend by watering her plants while she's away or help my partner by giving him a lift to the airport. That I really *should* lend a hand to my fellow cosplay enthusiast whose car has broken down by the side of the road. (And, hey, nice Wonder Woman costume by the way. Love the Lasso of Truth.)

Which type of reciprocity is most common? Typically, the closer two people become, the more likely they are to shift from personal, explicitly negotiated exchanges— the safest form of reciprocity when you don't know how much to trust someone—to relational or collective reciprocity, through bonds of attachment or team identity.

Of course, awkwardness can arise when two people read their reciprocity type differently. For example, when one person sees it as personal, and the other, relational, direct exchange propositions can be off-putting and cause conflict, damaging the relationship itself. I still remember when someone I thought of as a friend asked me if I would watch her cat when she went on vacation, which I was happy to do, *until* she offered me $100 to do it. I felt both extremely uncomfortable and just slightly insulted that she felt I would want compensation for doing her a favor. I thought we were *past that*, so to speak. I still watched the cat, of course, but I didn't really take any joy in it.

And that's the downside of inadvertently making people feel obligated to help you: while enthusiastically and freely given help confers a host of benefits on the helper, the people who give a grudging yes experience none of them. They may even start avoiding you, to avoid the pain of declining (or ignoring) your requests.

Avoidance is how we get around the dilemma of feeling controlled by other people's requests for help. Let's face it, this is something most of us have done at one time or another. When I was a graduate student and money was tight, I will admit to having deliberately avoided my fair share of Salvation Army Santas and school kids selling candy bars door-to-door. I have crossed the street to avoid anyone with a clipboard who looked suspiciously as if they were going to tell me about their worthy cause. To this day, I refuse all offers of assistance in stores for fear that if someone is nice to me, I will feel as if I have to buy something.

It doesn't make you bad person; it's just human nature. In one study, researchers told participants that they could answer a few questions about their upcoming Thanksgiving plans and be paid for doing so. They told half that, at the end, they'd offer the participants the choice between keeping the money and donating it to St. Jude's Children's Hospital. For this group, participation rates dropped by over 10 percent. When faced with a choice between keeping the money and feeling like a jerk, or giving away the money but feeling controlled, some people will choose to walk away altogether.[12]

It Helps to Remember

- Help seekers have to navigate a tricky paradox. Although researchers have found that there are loads of psychic benefits to being helpful—it makes helpers feel really, really good—those benefits evaporate when someone feels *compelled* to help.

- While some commonly used influence tactics—like asking people, "Can I ask you a favor?" before you actually ask the favor—do increase people's likelihood of helping, they come at a cost. They make us feel trapped, and so they reduce the quality or amount of help we give.

- Reciprocity would seem to be the answer; I help you, you help me, and we all walk away feeling good. But even accepting help from another person can make us feel controlled, as if we'll owe that person something.

- This is, if not bad news, then at least complicated news for help seekers.

Chapter 5

The Four Steps to Getting the Help You Need

You are walking down a city street on your way to work and notice an elderly man, seemingly asleep on a bench with a newspaper open on his lap. About a block later, you pass a young woman in a parked car. She is attempting to start the engine, but it won't turn over. A few feet away, a middle-aged woman with a fanny pack and a camera hanging around her neck keeps glancing back and forth between the map in her hands and the building numbers and street signs that surround you.

Once you arrive at work, you notice a colleague heading to his desk, trying to balance a box full of files under one arm without spilling his coffee. Your office mate gives you a quick hello and returns to frowning at her computer screen, muttering softly under her breath about how she can't make sense of the spreadsheet she's working on. On your voice mail is a message from a friend who wants to meet up for an after-work drink, and something about his tone in the message seems a bit off. But you've got a report due tomorrow, so you send him a quick text asking to reschedule.

Some of these people needed your help; others were just fine without it. If the events I just described happened in real life, do you think you would have known which was which?

The correct answer is: probably not. Practically speaking, it can be very, very difficult to recognize when someone needs help. Chances are good that you have witnessed events like the ones described countless times. Many of them probably didn't even consciously register in your mind, but you noticed them at least unconsciously. And, on some level, you made a decision about whether or not they required your attention. More often than not, you continued about your day, not because you are a selfish and unkind person, but because when situations are ambiguous, human beings tend to err on the side of minding their own damn business.

What this means is that when you yourself need help or support, it is—without question—far less obvious to the people around you than you think it is. Your colleague's cold indifference to your epic spreadsheet struggle, the rude New Yorkers who rush past you as you search in vain for the place that sells half-priced tickets to *The Lion King*—these people probably aren't indifferent or rude at all. They simply *don't see your need*.

Which brings us to the very first step in getting the help or support you desire. You have to make sure other people notice what is happening. But, of course, that's far from the only challenge: there are, in fact, four vital steps that must occur in order for a helper to ultimately help you.

Step 1: The Helper Needs to Notice That You Might Need Help

Obstacle: People Don't Attend to Everything Happening around Them

Human beings are, as a rule, preoccupied by their own affairs. We don't pay attention to every detail of our surroundings—including the other people in those surroundings—in no small part because it would be impossible to do so. There is just too much to take in. So we are selective, focusing first and foremost on those pieces of information that seem relevant to our own goals. This leads to a fascinating but pervasive phenomenon known as *inattentional blindness*, the most famous example of which is something called the Invisible Gorilla test.

Psychologists Dan Simons and Christopher Chabris (authors of the fascinating and aptly named book *The Invisible Gorilla*) asked participants in a study to watch a video of groups of people passing a basketball back and forth, and told them to count the number of passes made. At one point, a person in a full gorilla suit walks through the scene, but does not interact with the ball. When asked at the end of the video if they had witnessed anything out of the ordinary, 50 percent of participants said no. They had *completely failed to notice the gorilla* because they were so preoccupied with the task of counting passes.

Other studies have subsequently shown that, more generally, when people are focused on a particular goal or task, or when there is a high degree of *perceptual load* (i.e., lots of sights and sounds competing for attention), inattentional blindness is likely. This is why in busy or noisy environments—like major cities—people are less likely to notice that someone needs help and consequently are less likely to offer it than they are in quieter, more rural areas.[1] New Yorkers aren't necessarily less friendly, but they *are* bombarded by a constant stream of sights and sounds that the average person in Twin Lakes, Minnesota, just isn't subjected to. And if 50 percent of people can miss a guy in a gorilla suit in plain view, what are the odds that your office mate will notice that you could use a hand with that box of files?

It's not just a booming and buzzing environment that can make your need for help difficult for someone else to detect. Sometimes, the problem comes from within potential helpers themselves. Studies show, for instance, that people in negative moods—those who feel anxious, depressed, or frustrated—are less likely to pay attention to others around them or notice others' needs.[2] Similarly, being in a position of relative power over others, as managers are with respect to their employees, has been shown to direct one's attention away from the less powerful and toward one's own goals.[3] Ironically, it is, of course, the more powerful among us to whom we often look for help—and who have the greatest means with which to help—who are the very people least likely to notice that we are in trouble in the first place.

Step 2: The Helper Needs to Believe That You Desire Help

Obstacle: People Are Not Mind Readers

Sometimes, others fail to offer help not because they don't notice something is wrong, but because of what psychologists call *audience inhibition*—our general fear of looking foolish in front of other people.[4] In the case of helping, there are two main sources of inhibition. First, we worry that we might have misconstrued the situation (*perhaps that person flailing about in the pool just has a really awkward swimming technique* . . .) and will suffer the sting of embarrassment if we are wrong. Second, we also know that people can get very testy when you offer them unsolicited support; after all, just because someone is struggling, doesn't mean that they aren't still determined to rise to the challenge on their own. Even when it's crystal clear that a person could benefit from help, it doesn't necessarily mean that they *want* it.

Let's start with the first source of inhibition: How do people determine whether the need for help is genuine, when no one is yelling, "Please help me"? The answer is: we look around at the other potential helpers to see how *they* are reacting. If we see others readying to take action or even looking concerned, it validates our sense that something is genuinely wrong. But when other people *don't* react—when they are calm and continue to just go about their business—then we typically don't react either. The extent to which that last statement holds true is somewhat extraordinary.

Take, for example, a famous set of studies by Princeton University's Bibb Latane and John Darley from the 1960s. They told students to sit in a room and fill out questionnaires—either alone, or with two other students who were actually confederates in the experiment. After a while, smoke began to pour into the room through a vent. When the participant was alone, they would quickly become alarmed and seek out help. But when the participant was with two students who ignored the smoke completely, they did *nothing*. The smoke got thick enough that it actually became difficult to even *see* the questionnaires, but the participant stayed put, having inferred from the nonreactions of the other students that there was no cause for alarm. In a similar study, participants also failed to respond to screams and cries of pain from a woman in an adjoining room if the confederates appeared to not notice it.[5]

On some level, it makes sense that we look to other people to help us understand ambiguous situations, and yet on another level, it's utterly terrifying. More often than not, there is no reason to believe that the other people in question have superior knowledge or some unique insight into the situation. And yet we behave as if they do, trusting a collective wisdom that could just as easily turn out to be collective stupidity.

Now let's turn to the second source of audience inhibition: fearing that help may not be wanted. Apart from the very real concern that the beneficiary may have wanted to solve the problem on their own, there are also strong *norms*, or unwritten rules, in a society that can influence whether they will see the help as welcome. Perhaps the most widely known of these is the *norm of family privacy*, which makes people reluctant to interfere in domestic matters between, for example, husbands and wives, or parents and their children.

A frightening example of this norm in action comes from a study by Lance Shotland and Margaret Straw in the early 1970s. They staged a public physical assault by a man on a woman in front of both male and female witnesses. When the woman yelled, "I don't know you!" 65 percent of the bystanders stepped in to try to halt the attack. But when she yelled, "I don't know why I married you!" only 19 percent intervened.[6]

What happens when the relationship between the man and woman is unclear? In a separate study, over two-thirds of participants who watched a silent film that showed a man attacking a woman *assumed* that they were lovers or spouses, even though nothing in the film suggested this was the case. In other words, the norm of family privacy may interfere with getting help to someone in need even when there is no familial relationship to keep private.

Part of the problem is that generally speaking, people assume that if you want help, you will ask for it. They expect *you* to come to *them*, forgetting how uncomfortable and embarrassing it can be to ask for help, and how reluctant most of us are to do it. (In one study, for instance, researchers asked teaching assistants at the start of a semester how many students they thought would approach them for help throughout the course.

They overestimated help seeking by anywhere from 20 percent to 50 percent.[7])

Both the danger of misinterpretation and the fear that help will be unwelcome create significant obstacles for potential helpers. When you are the person in need, it is in your best interest to remove these obstacles, and the good news is that the means to removing them is entirely straightforward: *ask for help directly.*

I know that this may not be what you want to hear. We would all prefer if others could just intuit our need accurately and offer up help accordingly. But that's not how it works. When other people are walking around assuming that you would ask for help if you needed it, then actually asking is pretty much your only option.

The vast majority of prosocial behavior occurs, not surprisingly, in response to specific requests for assistance.[8] In the workplace, estimates suggest that as much as 75 percent to 90 percent of the help colleagues give one another is in response to direct appeals.[9] And nearly half of Americans who volunteer with charities and other public works say that they became involved as a result of having been asked by the organization itself or by a friend, family member, or coworker who also volunteered.[10]

Asking for help directly solves the obstacles of both step 1 and step 2—when you are proactive about making your need clear, your potential benefactor is both more likely to notice it and more likely to feel confident that help is welcome.

Step 3: The Helper Needs to Take Responsibility for Helping

Obstacle: Lots of People Could Help—Why Me?

If you have ever taken a social psychology course, you have heard the terrible, tragic story of Kitty Genovese. Though the story didn't quite happen the way it was initially reported, that initial reporting was the inspiration for research that led to one of our field's most important—and troubling—insights into why people do (and don't) help.[11]

Returning home to her apartment in Queens after work on an early March morning in 1964, the twenty-eight-year-old Genovese was brutally attacked and murdered by Walter Moseley, a twenty-nine-year-old machine operator. The attack took place in the courtyard of her apartment building over the course of a half-hour, during which Genovese cried out for help multiple times. That's not in dispute. The part that is disputed—and that led so many people to be horrified by the *New York Times* account of the murder—is that the police claimed that although many people had heard her cries for help, and even witnessed part of the attack, no one came to her aid.[12] More recent research suggests that many people did not hear or witness the crime, and of those who did, two called the police, one shouted at the assailant and scared him off, and another came out to cradle the dying Genovese in her arms.[13]

For years, the death of Kitty Genovese was cited as evidence of the extreme indifference and callousness of New Yorkers, too uncaring to bother to help a dying woman on their very doorstep. More recently, it's been called an example of police apathy—toward violence against women, or toward violence in certain neighborhoods. The horror of the story—as initially and sloppily reported—inspired numerous books, movies, and podcasts, and many fictional adaptations. It's also led to a large body of academic research on the *bystander effect*.

Researchers Latane and Darley were the first to theorize that it wasn't callousness or ignorance that stopped people from helping; they argued that there were *too many* potential helpers.

Imagine you are driving down an isolated back road in the countryside, and you pass an elderly woman stranded by the side of the road with her car's emergency blinkers on. Would you stop to help? Chances are good that you would, because you'd know that there might not be another car driving along this road for hours. If you don't help her, maybe no one will.

Now imagine you are driving down a busy city street and pass this same elderly woman with her car blinkers on. Would you stop to help her now? Almost certainly not, because, after all, with so many other people around, why should *you* be the one to help? Latane and Darley coined the term *diffusion of responsibility* to capture the difference between these two scenarios. The more people there are who *could* help, the less clear it is to everyone involved who *should* help.

To test their theory, they set up an elaborate experiment. Participants were seated alone in a room with a microphone. They were led to believe that they would be speaking to one to five other participants in a private conversation that the experimenters would not overhear. In reality, there were no other people in the experiment. Instead, each heard the same scripted version of another participant—who had mentioned having epilepsy—suddenly begin to have a seizure. He asked for help and then went silent.

When participants believed that they were the only person who heard what had happened, 100 percent sought help. But when they thought that a third person had heard it, only 80 percent sought help, and when they thought six people had, only 60 percent did so.

Latane and Darley also noticed that even when people did not seek help, they were far from complacent about it. Participants in the three- and six-person groups generally took longer to get help, and appeared visibly confused and agitated, unsure of how to behave in a situation where their own role was unclear. *Perhaps someone else has already gone for help? Should I do something, or just wait and see?*[14]

Subsequent studies show the same consistent effect—the more bystanders there are when someone is in need, the less likely anyone actually offers to help. It's not callousness; it's confusion about who, exactly, bears responsibility. I know you may need help, but why should it be me who gives it?

One of the most common ways in which people fall victim to diffusion of responsibility in their day-to-day lives is by making a classic error: asking for help via group email. There is nothing quite like being blind-copied on a request for support to make you feel less compelled to actually offer it. How many others are you asking to promote your product, review your book, or lend a hand with your new initiative? Dozens? Hundreds? If you can't bother to make an appeal to me directly for my aid, then clearly it's because you have so very many people who could offer you the same support. Frankly, I couldn't be *less* responsible for helping you if I tried.

So when you are seeking support, be aware that you will need to alleviate that confusion by giving your benefactor a clear sense of responsibility about helping you. Take the time to ask individuals directly and to send unique, personal emails when you need a hand. Otherwise, you will be far too easy to ignore.

Step 4: The Helper Needs to Be Able to Provide the Help You Need

Obstacle: Competing Commitments Can Be an Issue

You are, no doubt, a busy person. You may have a calendar bursting with appointments and a to-do list roughly a mile long. You may shudder to think about the sheer number of responsibilities on your plate and, consequently, avoid doing so as much as possible. So when someone asks you for a favor or some form of support, even when you would genuinely like to help, you may find yourself reluctant to agree to do so. Busy, hurried people routinely say no to things swiftly, without stopping to consider whether they might be able to reprioritize or squeeze in an additional commitment. They do this not because they are lazy or selfish, but because being busy literally taxes their brains. Having to think about many things at once or having to work within tight deadlines shrinks our working memory, limits our attention, and forces us to take mental shortcuts rather than thinking things through.

And there is perhaps no better example of the effect of busyness in action than a study of Princeton seminary students who were asked to give a talk on the parable of the Good Samaritan.

In case you aren't familiar with the parable:

> "And who is my neighbor?" Jesus replied, "A man was going down from Jerusalem to Jericho, and he fell among robbers, who stripped him and beat him, and departed, leaving him half dead. Now by chance a priest was going down the road; and when he saw him he passed by on the other side. So likewise a Levite, when he came to the place and saw him, passed by on the other side. But a Samaritan, as he journeyed, came to where he was; and when he saw him, he had compassion, and went to him and bound his wounds, pouring on oil and wine; then he set him on his own beast and brought him to an inn, and took care of him. And the next day he took out two dennarii and gave them to the innkeeper, saying, 'Take care of him; and whatever more you spend, I will repay you when I come back.' Which of these three, do you think, proved neighbor to him who fell among the robbers?" He said, "The one who showed mercy on him." And Jesus said to him, "Go and do likewise."[15]

Researchers John Darley and Daniel Batson invited seminary students at Princeton to participate in a study on "religious education and vocations." The seminarians began the study in one building, where they filled out a series of questionnaires. The researchers then asked them to report to another building all the way across campus for the second part of the study, where they would have to give a talk. They told half that the talk would be on the kinds of jobs for which seminary students are best suited; they asked the other half to share and expand upon the parable of the Good Samaritan.

Finally, they put half of the seminarians into a busy, high-pressure state. Just before leaving, the experimenter looked at his wristwatch and said, "Oh, you're late. They were expecting you a few minutes ago. We'd better get moving. The assistant should be waiting for you so you'd better hurry. It should take just a minute."

Traveling between the buildings, each passed, in plain view, a "victim" slumped over in an alleyway with his eyes closed. As the participant went by, the victim coughed twice and groaned, keeping his head down.

Given that these were not just the typical undergraduates who participate in psychology experiments, but *seminary* students—devoted to the learning and practice of religious principles—what percentage do you think stopped to engage with and offer help to the victim?

Overall, 60 percent of the participants offered the victim *no form of help* whatsoever. And among those who were told that they were running late and should hurry, only 10 percent offered help.

But what about the participants who were told that they would be talking about the Good Samaritan, literally *right before* encountering the victim? Surely, after being primed with thoughts of compassion and generosity, wouldn't they be more likely to notice and respond to his need?

Wrong again. The topic of the talk they would give had *no impact whatsoever* on the likelihood of helping. As Darley and Batson noted, "Indeed, on several occasions, a seminary student going to give his talk on the parable of the Good Samaritan literally stepped over the victim as he hurried on his way!"[16] (I have always found that comment both horrifying and hilarious to picture.)

Assuming you are not lying groaning in a doorway and simply need common everyday help, it's essential to remember when you ask for it that people are very often quite busy; they have their own goals to juggle and fires to put out. You can make receiving help from a busy person more likely by doing three things.

First, be *explicit and detailed* about what you are asking for and how much effort from the helper it will entail. Vague requests to "connect with you about your work" or "get a hand from you with something" are likely to leave people worrying that the ask is going to be signif-icant, and that they just won't have the time and energy for it. Second, be mindful to keep requests for help to a *reasonable* size—something the other person can do, given other commitments. And third, be *open* to receiv-ing help that is different from what you asked for. Don't get hung up on not getting what you wanted. Focus instead on how you are strengthening your relationship by taking the help that *is* offered, and bear in mind that it might be far more useful to you than you realize.

Let's sum up. To provide assistance, your benefactor must notice your need and believe that you desire help. You can make this easier by making direct, explicit requests for help. Don't beat around the bush. He or she also needs to take responsibility for helping, which tends to happen more when requests are made to one individ-ual specifically, rather than to a group at large. Last, your helper has a life, too. Make your request reasonable and clear, and be open to taking whatever help you can get.

It Helps to Remember

- The first step to getting the help you want from others is ensuring that they see your need. In general, people aren't paying attention to you the way you assume they are because they are preoccupied with their own stuff.

- You need to assure your potential benefactors that you welcome the help they could provide. People know that you might resent unrequested help, so you need to convey that you actually want help.

- Ensure that the potential helper actually assumes responsibility for helping. When you ask for help from a large group (say, via an email with many recipients), it's not clear why I should be the one to help you.

- Finally, remember that your need is not the only thing your helper has to worry about. People have other commitments. Be open to allowing them to help you in other ways, if they just can't manage your initial request.

Chapter 6

Don't Make It Weird

My friend Thomas Wedell-Wedellsborg, coauthor of *Innovation as Usual*, has helped me more times than I can count. I've also seen him cheerfully say no to enough requests to know that like me, his generosity is not without limits. He recently told me about a time he'd helped someone, and the story stood out to me both for how well it illustrates the research findings on giving's benefits, and for his refreshing (though quite typical for Thomas) degree of candor on the subject:

> I'm flying back from a speaking gig in Singapore, and I meet in the airport a friend of my mother's who's been out visiting her son, who happens to live in Singapore. As I board the plane, I'm called first because I'm in business class, and I realize she's in economy class.

I go into the plane and look at the economy section—and I am selfish enough to ask myself, "Could I survive twelve hours here?" But I concluded that I could, so when she came onboard the plane, I said, "You've got the wrong ticket." I took her into my business-class seat and I took the twelve-hour ride in economy.

Now, when I did that, it was partially a calculated choice. Of course I wanted to make her happy . . . But another part of it was definitely the awareness that this would create positive repercussions back home in my mother's bridge club. "Oh, he's such a wonderful guy," and so on. So in part, my choice was egotistically motivated.

But here's the interesting thing. After giving her my seat and seeing how happy she became, I sat in economy with the biggest smile for an hour. I felt massive joy. I was really surprised by the intensity of my own joy in having done that, in being a person who did such a thing. There were two very happy people on the flight that day.

One of the most common misconceptions about giving is that, if you are doing it right, it's entirely about the other person. That giving is not supposed to be about you. But this is nonsense. The choice to help another person is often, if not always, at least in part about how you see yourself and how helping will make you feel. And this is a good thing, because the benefits of helping *to the helper* provide a powerful source of motivation, one so powerful that it can make a perfectly reasonable and intelligent man giddy about spending twelve hours in coach.

But just think how differently Thomas would have felt had his mother's friend realized he was in business class, walked up to him, and said, "Young Tommy, would you mind trading seats?"

Ways to Make It Weird

Asking for help is tricky because it isn't just about what you say and do. It's also about what you *don't* say or do. As we discussed in chapter 4, there's an inherent paradox in asking for help; just making the request can take away some of the intrinsic motivation of the potential helper. That said, there are some specific things you can say that can really backfire. In this chapter, we'll look at some of the most common ways well-intentioned people screw this up and make it weird for the helper.

Overdoing It on Empathy

Empathy is a powerful motivator of helping. It is elicited when we perceive someone or something in need, when we value their welfare, and most importantly, when we take their perspective—imagining what it would be like to be in their shoes. This in essence creates an at least temporary sense of shared collective reciprocity (the sense, discussed in chapter 4, that we'll help someone because we share something in common with them).

In empathy's case, the sense of reciprocity is based on a shared, *imagined* experience. We can understand what it *might feel like* to be stranded on the side of the road, be without clean clothes, or be unable to understand strange Swedish stick figures. And so we stop to help stranded motorists, do other people's laundry (even though *we really hate it*), and help our friends assemble their IKEA shelves.

The cool thing about empathy is that because it's based on imagination, we can have empathy for people we've never met, in situations we've never been in. We can even have empathy for people in situations that aren't possible. For example, moviegoers can feel intense concern for Matt Damon's astronaut in *The Martian*, even though we know it's not possible for Hollywood actors (or anyone else for that matter) to get to Mars, much less get stranded there. We can imagine it so vividly that we really wish we could do something to help.

In the right amounts, eliciting empathy can be a very effective way to obtain support. Until you take it too far, that is. Because "I feel your pain" stops working the moment the pain becomes too great. Then the person from whom you are trying to elicit empathy is quite likely to shut down entirely and try to get away from you as soon as possible, probably without helping at all.

The example I always think of in this case is a particular TV commercial from the American Society for the Prevention of Cruelty to Animals. Now, I love dogs. I've loved them all my life. I don't think it's possible to love them more than I do. Without exaggeration, my dream is to one day retire to one of those big farms where I can just let rescue dogs roam free, cared for in comparative doggie luxury. But I cannot *tolerate*, for more than about two seconds, the ASPCA commercial set to the soppy Sarah McLachlan song, "Angel." It is heartbreaking to see all those sad-eyed cats and dogs in cages, while quite possibly the most heart-wrenching song in human history plays in the background. And it's not just me; my two children (who are also crazy about animals) start screaming, "Turn it off! Turn it off!" when they hear the opening chord.

I donate to several animal rescue organizations, both local and national, including the ASPCA. But that commercial has done nothing to increase my generosity. If anything, it's made me wary of watching anything on the channels where it normally airs. And I'm sure I'm not the only one.

So use empathy as a help-seeking tool with caution, or it might achieve the opposite result you are looking for.

Apologizing Profusely

Have you ever had the (often very uncomfortable) experience of being showered with apologies while hearing a request for help? "I'm so sorry to ask you for this, Heidi, but I could really use your help with this assignment. It's terrible that I have to ask. I really should be able to do it myself, and I know you are so busy. I just really hate myself for asking." Ugh.

Getting a request like this feels awful. Of course you, like me, would probably say yes to it, in no small part just to get it over with. But this would fall firmly into the *controlled* helping category—*I'm doing this because I have to, not because I want to.*

Musician and former street performer Amanda Palmer, in her insightful book *The Art of Asking*, wrote at length about her experiences as an artist who sustained herself and her work by asking for donations. When giving advice to other artists, she said that she frequently admonished them to stop apologizing for their need, because (as she correctly noted) apologies are *distancing*.

It's understood, implicitly, that people who are on the same team—people who share a sense of relational or collective reciprocity—will lean on one another from time to time for support. And that, naturally, this support will be *reciprocated*. Apologies that accompany a request for help subtly imply that we must *not* be on the same team; otherwise, why would you be apologizing? In this sense, apologizing actually undermines our shared in-group identity, increasing the gap between us and severing our feelings of connectedness.

If you are asking for help because you've made a mess—you missed an important deadline or needlessly alienated a client—and now you need someone's help to clean up the mess, that's different. In that case, apologize for making the mess.

But in general, you should avoid apologizing for simply asking for help. Instead, make a request and offer appreciation when someone helps you. That's much more satisfying for everyone, all around.

Using Disclaimers

Often, those seeking help are so busy trying to establish that they are not personally weak or greedy that they turn the focus away from the helper and onto themselves. They say things like, "I'm not normally the type that asks for help . . ." or "I wouldn't ask you if I had a choice . . ." or even "I hate having to ask you for this . . ."

The impulse is understandable. Asking for help *is* uncomfortable. The people we're asking to lend us a hand *might* feel imposed upon. But using disclaimers like these is the wrong way to make it better. I can't get a lot of personal satisfaction from helping you if I know that you hated having to ask me, and that you appear to be miserable about the whole thing.

And just as we saw with collective or relational reciprocity, any attempt to make it transactional—*this is what's in it for you if you help me*—undermines my ability to see myself in a positive light for helping you.

So even if you are a bit uncomfortable about asking for help, try not to telegraph it to the help giver. Keep it positive and relaxed, and worry a little less about how you look and a little more about how they feel.

Emphasizing How Much the Other Person Will Love Helping

"You're going to love it! It will be so much fun!" One of my collaborators has a lifelong friend who has a habit of phrasing her requests for help this way.

"Any chance you could help me repaint the living room this weekend? We can totally drink beers and catch up! Girl time!" she might say. Or, "Hey, could you pick me up at the auto mechanic? I haven't seen you in ages! Road trip!"

It's a testament to the strength of their friendship that it survives this kind of request for help.

Don't ever try to explicitly convince someone else that they will find helping you rewarding. *Why?*, you might be wondering. *You've gone on and on about how helping* does *make people happy.*

It's true that helping makes people happy, but reminding people of this generally drains the joy out of helping. First, it reeks of manipulation and control, undermining the helper's sense of autonomy. Second, it's presumptive as all hell. *Don't tell me about how I'm going to feel, you big jerk. That's for me to decide.*

Now, it *is* OK to point out the benefits of helping if you can manage to be a bit more subtle about it—say, by making more general statements (e.g., "Donating is a way to give back to the community") rather than the focusing on the helper specifically. But be careful not to pile it on and mix egotistical reasons (self-benefits) with altruistic reasons (other-benefits), because it makes the manipulation particularly noticeable.[1]

For example, in one study, just under a thousand alumni who had never donated to their college were contacted by fund-raisers via email. There were three versions of the appeal: (1) egoistic: "Alumni report that giving makes them feel good," (2) altruistic: "Giving is your chance to make a difference in the lives of students, faculty, and staff," and (3) a combined appeal. Researchers found that both the self- and other-directed appeals were equally effective, but the combined appeal saw donation rates cut in half.

Portraying the Help You Need as a Tiny, Insignificant Favor

Because asking for help makes us so uncomfortable, and because we really do expect that people will say no, a common tactic is to portray the help we need as a small, piddling, almost invisible, negligible really, barely there, little favor. We might emphasize the overall lack of inconvenience helping us will cause, as in, "Could you drop these contracts off at the client's? It's practically on your way home." Or we might highlight how little time it will take the helper to help us: "Would you add these updates to the database? It probably won't take you more than five minutes." The thing is, by minimizing our request, we also minimize the helper's help and thus minimize any warm feelings the act of helping us might have generated.

There's also a not-insignificant risk that we have wildly miscalculated the size of the favor we're asking, especially if the person we're asking to help us does work we don't fully understand.

Every now and then, my book editor will get an email from an old friend asking her to take a look at something he's currently writing. Usually it's phrased as a small request, for example, "I think it's pretty clean; maybe just give it a quick proofread? It shouldn't take you very long!" When she opens the attachment, the item in question is invariably a six-thousand-word academic article. Except for the time it was a full-length monograph. Yes, an entire book.

The thing is, I don't think these help requestors are selfish. Just clueless. They have really no idea of the hours (and hours) of work they're asking her to do. Not understanding the work she does, they don't know how much a freelance editor would get paid to do it. What they're inadvertently doing is conveying to her that they think the work she does is easy, quick, trivial, and not very taxing. Not a great way to enlist her help.

Chances are you also work with people whose work you don't understand at all. The IT department, HR, compliance, sales, marketing—the people in these functions are almost always subject to muttered gripes about how rigid and slow they are, or how disorganized and wasteful. "What do they do all day?" is a common complaint. What, indeed? If you don't know, don't presume it doesn't take them very long.

Reminding People That They Owe You One

"Remember when I took over that really tough client of yours?"

"Remember the time I babysat your screaming child?"

"Remember how you always used to forget your house key, and I had to come home and let you in?"

Because we know how reciprocity works (chapter 4), and because asking for help makes us feel weak and icky, we might sometimes be tempted to remind the people we're asking how we've helped them in the past. This, too, is fraught with awkwardness.

For example, when my editor received that monograph in her inbox, she wanted to say no. She *deeply* wanted to say no. She hadn't really kept in touch with this old friend, and she had plenty of other ways she wanted to spend her weekend. But, for all the reasons that saying no is really painful, she felt she couldn't say no—not completely. So she wrote back, explained politely that he was asking her to do about forty hours of work, and asked him if there was one chapter he was particularly worried about. When he replied, he reminded her that he'd edited her writing, too, back when she was a sports columnist. In theory, this might make sense—he *had* done her a favor, and they were old friends, so it would make sense she'd do him a favor, right?

Not so much. While reciprocity does make people more likely to say yes to our requests for help, it can also make us feel controlled, which, you may remember, takes all the fun out of helping. Reciprocity works best when the acts of help are roughly *equal*—as editing a few five-hundred-word sports columns and editing a fifty-thousand-word historical treatise are not. They should also be *temporally proximate*; unless someone has done you a truly massive favor such as, say, saving your life, they won't feel they owe you anything ten years down the line. And they should tap into one of the specific types of reciprocity psychologists have identified: personal, relational, or collective.

For example, my editor is glad to edit articles for her neighbor, a carpenter who also writes how-to articles for do-it-yourself magazines, because her neighbor has helped her with projects around the house on numerous occasions. That's an example of personal reciprocity in action: the exchange is a fairly clear trade. She's also happy to edit her husband's essays on fly-fishing (relational reciprocity) and proofread the grad school application essay of her cousin's boyfriend, even though she doesn't know him very well (collective reciprocity).

The bottom line on reciprocity is this: if you have to remind someone that they owe you one, chances are they don't feel as if they do. *Reminding* them that they owe you a favor both makes the other person feel as if you're trying to control them (which, let's be honest, you kind of are) and elicits what Adam Grant calls "matching" behavior—it's not particularly generous, and it doesn't create good feeling. It's like going out for pizza with a friend, only to be told you should pay more since you ate two extra slices.

It makes the other person feel as if you're keeping a scorecard, and that kind of scorekeeping is fundamentally bad for relationships.

Talking about How Much Their Help Will Benefit You

You weren't raised in a barn (probably). You know you need to express gratitude and appreciation for other people's help. And yet people often make a critical mistake when expressing gratitude: they focus on how *they* feel—how happy they are, how they have benefited from the help—rather than focusing on the *benefactor*.

Researchers Sara Algoe, Laura Kurtz, and Nicole Hilaire at the University of North Carolina distinguished between two types of gratitude expressions: *other-praising*, which involves acknowledging and validating the character or abilities of the giver (i.e., their positive identity); and *self-benefit*, which describes how the receiver is better off for having been given help. In one of their studies, they observed couples expressing gratitude to one another for something their partner had recently done for them.[2] Their expressions were then coded for the extent to which they were other-praising or focused on self-benefit. Examples of their expressions included:

Other-praising

It shows how responsible you are . . .

You go out of your way . . .

I feel like you're really good at that.

Self-benefit

It let me relax.

It gave me bragging rights at work.

It makes me happy.

Finally, benefactors rated how responsive they felt the gratitude giver had been, how happy they felt, and how loving they felt toward their partner. The researchers found that other-praising gratitude was strongly related to perceptions of responsiveness, positive emotion, and loving, but self-benefit gratitude was *not*.

This is worth taking a moment to think about, because most people get gratitude utterly wrong. Human beings are, more often than not, a bit egocentric by nature. We have a tendency to talk about ourselves, even when we should be thinking and talking about others. So naturally, when we get high-quality help and support, we want to talk how it made *us* feel. Also, to be fair, we assume that that's what the helper wants to hear—that they were helping *to make us happy*, so therefore they must want to hear about how happy we are.

But this assumption isn't quite right. Yes, your helper wants you to be happy, no doubt, but the motivation to be helpful is intimately tied to the helper's identity and self-esteem. We help because we want to be good people—to live up to our goals and values, and admittedly, to be admired. Helpers want to see themselves positively, which is difficult for them to do when you won't stop talking about you.

Any Weird Request Can Be Made in a Non-Weird Way

There are really three ways of asking people for help that avoid making them feel controlled and that let them experience the natural high of helping. These three reinforcements create the desire to want to help another; you can use them in specific requests for help, and you can learn to emphasize them to create a culture of helpfulness. The coming chapters will focus in depth on each.

The first reinforcement is what psychologists call a strong sense of *in-group*. In other words, the belief that the person in need is on your team—a part of a group that is important to you. This goes beyond mere collective reciprocity; we help people from our in-group because we *care* about what happens to the in-group. Because our own happiness and well-being are affected by the group's happiness and well-being. People routinely (and voluntarily) risk their lives for family members, fellow soldiers, police officers, or firefighters because of the strength of their in-group bonds. Helping to create (or to highlight) the in-group status of a person in need reliably leads to a genuine desire to help.

The second reinforcer is the opportunity for *positive identity*. In other words, when helping you *makes me feel good about me*. Particularly when it allows me to see myself as possessing a positive attribute or playing an admired role. For example, people help more when they reflect on why it's important to them to "be a *benefactor* to others." When a positive identity—like being a benefactor—is made salient, people are more likely to act in accordance with it. In one instance, it increased the number of calls per hour among volunteer fund-raisers by roughly 30 percent. In another, volunteer callers who reflected on being benefactors increased their donation rates to earthquake relief through the American Red Cross from 21 percent to 46 percent.

The last reinforcer—and the most powerful one of the three—is the opportunity to see one's own *effectiveness*. In other words, people want to see or know the impact of the help they have given or will give. They want to see it land. This is actually not an ego thing. It's what some psychologists have argued is *the* fundamental human motivation: to feel effective. To know that your actions create the results you intended. To, in essence, shape the world around you. In the absence of feedback—when we have no idea what the consequences of our actions have been—motivation takes a nosedive. And that is particularly true when it comes to helping.

These three reinforcements determine whether or not the desire to help you will arise intrinsically in your helper. Without them, they *might* still help you, but the benefits of that help will be yours alone. The help you receive will be more limited, and over time, the relationship you have with the helper may suffer.

Often, the potential for these reinforcers is already there—the in-group status, the potential for positive identity, a way for them to see their help land. But then we ruin it by saying the wrong thing when making a request or being thoughtless about the follow-up. In part III, I'll show you how to provide these essential reinforcers to your helpers when asking for help.

It Helps to Remember

- Asking for help is tricky because it isn't just about what you say and do. It's also about what you *don't* say or do. There are lots of ways to weird people out when you ask them for help.

- Apologizing profusely, using disclaimers, minimizing the nature of the request, and reminding people that they owe you a favor are all common ways that help seekers inadvertently alienate the people they need help from. Even talking a lot about how much you'd appreciate someone's help can backfire. You're making it all about you.

- When you ask for help, focus on the things that reinforce helpful behavior: a sense of being part of a shared purpose, a positive sense of identity, and the ability to see the effectiveness of one's help in action.

Part Three

Creating a Culture of Helpfulness

Chapter 7

The In-Group
Reinforcement

The human brain is social by nature. It evolved to successfully navigate a world populated by predators and prey, but more importantly, by *other humans*. Consequently, we pay more attention to information about other people than we do about anything else and process that information using a distinct set of brain networks.

There is even a region of the brain's temporal lobe that is dedicated specifically to recognizing people's faces, but there are no specialized regions for recognizing types of dogs, fruits, or automobiles. (Incidentally, damage that part of the temporal lobe and you may suffer from prosopagnosia, or "face blindness," a frustrating disorder that renders you incapable of recognizing anyone from their face alone. People with prosopagnosia are often forced to use secondary cues, like someone's voice, gait, or even hair color to identify them. But I digress.)

Why is so much of the brain's time and energy spent on other people? Human beings are acutely attuned to signals of belonging (as we discussed in chapter 1) because being part of a group of other humans is and has always been essential for our survival. But more than that, as about fifty years of social psychology research has shown, group membership is an essential component of our identity. It contributes in large part to our sense of who we are and what we're all about.

Ultimately, understanding group membership, and when and why we see other people as members of our group (or not), is essential because it is one of the single best predictors of who is and is not likely to help you. Human beings are simply wired to help their own tribe. It's in our DNA because it helped keep those skinny, hairless packs of fangless apes alive and well through the millions of years we existed without weapons, hospitals, or 911.

The preference for helping others in your own group emerges in early childhood. Studies show that preschoolers share more with friends (to the extent they share at all), and children as young as five judge it more favorable (and more emotionally satisfying) to help family members than strangers. Children are even more likely to help others from their own school, their own community, and their own race.[1] Of course, these tendencies continue into adulthood, as people generally prefer to help members of their own communities, including the colleges they attended.[2]

This preference for our own group can lead to all sorts of unfairness and bias in supposedly meritocratic systems. But once you understand how the psychology of groups works, you can counteract the unfair aspects of this and learn to strategically emphasize certain groups over others to make the groups you share with other people what psychologists call "salient" (e.g., relevant and noticeable) so that they'll be more likely to help you. As a manager, you can use simple techniques to make your team feel like a real group, so that your employees will feel a natural sense of helpfulness toward one another. (And no, there won't be any trust falls or ropes courses involved.)

You Look Like a _____

In America, usually the first question a stranger will ask you at a cocktail party is "So, what do you do?" But well before you hear them speak those words, the stranger's brain has asked—and answered—a different question about you: *What groups do you belong to?* Part of our initial processing of information about another person involves immediately and automatically categorizing them—largely unconsciously—into social categories (e.g., male, Hispanic, lawyer, etc.).

The social categories, or groups, to which we belong can be something we choose or something we are born into. They are created by common characteristics, behaviors, or beliefs. And the groups the brain categorizes you in are usually socially meaningful, like race, gender, nationality, age, political party, occupation, and so on.

Senior citizens are a group. So are car salesmen, Buddhists, women, lesbians, Tea Party activists, nudists, and soccer moms. Knowing that a person belongs to one of these groups tells you something about them because of what they have in common, though it probably tells you a lot less than you (at least unconsciously) assume. More on that in a minute.

Having any old thing in common with another person, however, doesn't necessarily make you a group. If I just happen to be walking around the same department store as you, that doesn't mean much. We tend to categorize people into groups according to more significant attributes, ones that we believe tell us something about who they are and what they are likely to think, feel, and do.

Ultimately, the reason we do all of this is a very practical one. Putting things—not just people, but also other stuff—into categories is essential for human beings to get around in the world successfully. Imagine if every time you encountered a new object or person, you had *literally no idea* what it was or how to interact with it. You would walk into a room and see a whole bunch of objects with four legs connected by a squarish piece of material, with another squarish piece attached to that one at a ninety-degree angle, and without the category "chair" to put them into, you wouldn't know if these objects were for sitting, climbing, or eating.

But once I identify this object as being a "chair," I know immediately what it's for and what to expect from it. The same is true for categories like traffic light, bagel, and polar bear. They fill in the blanks for us, allowing us to know something about things we've never encountered before and guiding our behavior toward them. It may be the first time I've encountered this *particular* polar bear, but armed with knowledge of the category to which it belongs, I know not to try to cuddle with it.

Group membership is a people category, and just like the polar bear, knowing that you are a police officer, or a grandmother, or an escaped felon tells me something about what I can (probably) expect from you, and how I should (probably) interact with you. I might be wrong, but at least I'm not just guessing wildly. Which is why categorizing people into groups is something the brain has evolved to do automatically and effortlessly, often below our conscious awareness.

We extract information about the groups to which others belong not only from physical cues like skin color or uniform, but from other things that might signal group membership, like names. This is particularly problematic when it comes to hiring, as reviewers can be subtly influenced by the name on a résumé, rather than focusing exclusively on the applicant's skills and experience. For example, one study showed that employers were 50 percent more likely to invite "Kristen Jones" for an interview after reading her résumé than "LaToya Jones," even when the two résumés were *identical*, because of the racial groups that employers assumed each candidate belonged to.[3]

Which brings us to the very obvious downside of categorizing people into groups. Human beings often— almost always unconsciously—rely on stereotypes (positive *and* negative) of groups to make judgments about individual members. Which would be fine if (1) stereotypes were always accurate, and (2) every member of the group was exactly like every other member. And since it's painfully obvious that both of those statements aren't true, we draw the wrong conclusions about others, particularly those we have just met, fairly regularly.

In addition, if the person you meet sees you as belonging to a different group, one that they themselves don't belong to, then you may be in real trouble. Out-group members are judged more negatively, and we rely on stereotypes and generalizations to understand them far more than we do members of our own group, the in-group.

Are You In or Out?

Being a part of another person's in-group can be a very, very good thing. As I mentioned, historically it's been essential for our very survival. Going it alone in the wilderness is not a great idea for a relatively hairless and skinny creature without fangs or claws to defend itself. Even the people on *Naked and Afraid* get a partner, right?

But the benefits of group membership go well beyond not being eaten by wolves. They give us a sense of belonging and connectedness. Fellow group members help us to feel understood and appreciated, because we sometimes share the same challenges and frustrations. They give us a sense of security, both physical and psychological. And, of course, working together, they allow us to achieve things we couldn't possibly achieve alone.

Groups also give us more to celebrate. We can bask in the reflected glow of our fellow group members' achievements, even when technically they are not our own. (When you hear middle-aged, overweight football fans say things like, "*We* played a great game last night," that's the sort of reflected glow I'm talking about.)

Of course, groups also bring with them the potential for tension *between* them, and prejudice and discrimination against out-group members. Here are but a few examples of what researchers have found in more than fifty years of studying how people perceive members of the out-group:

You people. People are more likely to see in-group members as unique individuals, while painting out-group members with a broader brush, relying more on generalizations and stereotyping that suggest that out-group members are all the same.

Apples and oranges. While differences among groups do certainly, on average, exist, they tend to be significantly exaggerated. For example, stereotypes about men and women in most cultures wildly overestimate the actual differences between the groups on dimensions like assertiveness or talkativeness.[4] That "men are from Mars, women are from Venus" stuff is mostly nonsense. We're all from Earth, and our similarities far outnumber our differences.

All redheads have bad tempers. When a member of your own in-group engages in some unusual activity—say, getting into a drunken bar brawl, or robbing a gas station, or chaining themselves to a tree to protest deforestation—you probably wouldn't say to yourself, "Yeah, I guess we're all like that." But when an out-group member does it, well, that's a different story. Then, we tend to fall victim to something psychologists call *illusory correlation*—seeing a relationship between two things (e.g., the group to which someone belongs, and their drunken bar brawling) when they are, in fact, unrelated.

Well, this is awkward. Interactions with out-group members are more arousing and provoke more anxiety and other negative emotions. Even anticipating such an interaction can create these emotional responses. Implicitly, we feel less at ease with members of out-groups than we do our own tribe of similar others. Explicitly, we may worry that the interaction will be awkward or unpleasant. Which, ironically, tends to lead to something of a self-fulfilling prophecy. If I expect you, as an out-group member, to behave with hostility toward me, then I am likely to (unconsciously) brace for that hostility and, in so doing, behave in ways that actually elicit hostility or, at a minimum, significant discomfort for both of us.

Every effect I just described can, in theory, be mitigated when people approach interactions with a strong, conscious intent to avoid out-group bias and perceive others fairly and accurately. But doing so takes significant cognitive effort. Which means that these effects are all exacerbated when the perceiver is under any kind of time pressure, cognitive load from thinking about many things at once, or experiencing strong emotions like fear or frustration that interfere with mental processing. Think of the last time you weren't experiencing *any* of these three things. ("When I was asleep" doesn't count.) And now, I think, you see the problem.

Interestingly, while other primates show group-based prosocial behavior, humans are unique in that these effects extend to anonymous in-group members—in other words, to strangers.[5] Of course, socially meaningful groups, created by shared goals or experiences, or significant similarities, form the basis for the strongest sense of in-group. But humans, unlike chimpanzees or gorillas, appear to be willing to accept a much broader view of what constitutes justification for you being "one of us," frankly, at times, to the point of silliness.

Some of the most well-known and cited studies in psychology are those that Henri Tajfel, inventor of the *minimal group paradigm*, conducted in the 1960s and 1970s. The idea of a "minimal group" is pretty much exactly what it sounds like: What is the minimum you need to do in order to instill people with the sense that they are part of a specific in-group? The answer is, not much. Tajfel and his colleagues were able to create functioning in-groups by doing things like:

- Asking people to guess the number of dots on a screen. He then randomly told some that they were "overestimators" and others that they were "underestimators."

- Showing people abstract paintings and asking them to evaluate them. He randomly told some that based on their answers, they were fans of the artist Paul Klee. He told the others that they preferred Wassily Kandinsky. (Most participants had never heard of either artist.)

The groups that he created had no shared history or shared goals. All they had in common were relatively meaningless personality traits or preferences. But despite that, Tajfel's studies showed that participants would, when later given the opportunity, reliably allocate more rewards, like money or candy, to people in their own groups. The desire to help our own is strong and can reveal itself in the unlikeliest of places.[6]

But *why* do we go out of our way to help the in-group? As I mentioned before, there are clear evolutionary pressures here. Why the odds of human survival go way up when wanting to be helpful to members of our tribe is baked into our source code. Groups thrive when individual members eschew what is best for them personally and focus on tending to the group in times of need.[7] But is that all that's going on?

Almost certainly not. Because as I mentioned earlier, group membership makes up a significant part of our identity—of who we think we are. And identity is kind of a big deal. (A lot more on that in the next chapter.) Research suggests that helping other group members is inherently satisfying because we are motivated to sustain the group to protect and enhance our own identities (e.g., when women help other women in order to promote the advancement of women as a group in society).

For example, psychologists Leor Hackel, Jamil Zaki, and Jay Van Bavel used fMRI (or functional magnetic resonance imaging) to study brain responses when participants observed both in-group and out-group members win money. Before the experiment began, they asked participants to indicate how "invested" they were in their group—in this case, fellow New York University students. Specifically, they asked the participants whether being an NYU student was "an important part of my identity," and the extent to which they felt "similar" to other NYU students. (The out-group students were from Columbia University, also located in New York City.)

The researchers found that the strength of the students' identification with NYU directly predicted the intensity of brain responses to in-group members winning money in the ventral striatum and medial prefrontal cortex, two areas associated with the processing of reward experiences. Even though they themselves weren't winning anything, the brain literally registered it as a win. But they observed no such effect for out-group members. Watching Columbia University students win money, frankly, didn't "do it" for them.[8]

We can see these same effects in real life, when we look at prosocial behavior in the workplace. Studies show that employees help more at work when they have a stronger sense of belonging and connection with their coworkers.[9]

Going from Out to In

No wonder the world at times seems to be in such a sorry state. Out-group bias can drive a whole host of inaccuracies in how we perceive one another, creating unnecessary animosity and pushing us further and further apart.

But group membership isn't just a source of discrimination against out-group members. It can, under the right circumstances, be a means to bridging the gaps that divide us.

One frequently replicated experiment asks individuals to identify words as either positive (e.g., puppy, flower, sunshine) or negative (e.g., vomit, garbage, suffering) as quickly as possible when they appear on the computer screen. Before each word appears, a face flashes on the screen for a split second. White participants are reliably faster at correctly identifying words as positive when they are paired with in-group (white) faces and reliably slower when they are paired with out-group (black) faces.

So depressing, right? But psychologists Jay Van Bavel and Will Cunningham at Ohio State University ran this experiment again, this time with an important difference. Before doing the word-categorization task, the researchers showed participants a group of photographs on a table, divided into two groups. Each group comprised *both* white and black faces—the same faces they would later see in the computer task. They told participants that one of the groups was made up of the members of *their* team—the people with whom they would be working on a later task—and that the other group of faces was the *opposing* team. After briefly looking at the photos, the participants went on to identify words as positive or negative when paired with the faces.

The results were somewhat astounding. The effect of race essentially disappeared, and instead, participants were faster at identifying words as positive when paired with members of their own team—*regardless of race*—and slower with members of the opposing team.[10]

In other words, race is one of many ways our brains may categorize people. But we can emphasize other categories—like being on the same team, or working together toward the same goal—and make the brain switch to using *that* as the basis for concluding who is in and who is out.

You probably don't need your colleagues to help you categorize a bunch of meaningless photographs. But you do need them to help you do something. How can you use the research on group psychology to foster the helpful behavior of others?

Use the Word "Together"

I know, this sounds almost unbelievably cheesy. But new research by Priyanka Carr and Greg Walton of Stanford University shows that simply saying the word "together" can have powerful motivational effects. In Carr and Walton's studies, participants first met in small groups and then separated to work on difficult puzzles on their own. People in the *psychologically together* category were told that they would be working on their task together even though they would be in separate rooms, and would either write to or receive a tip from a team member to help them solve the puzzle later on. In the *psychologically alone* category, there was no mention of being together, and the tip they would write or receive would come from the researchers. All the participants were, in fact, working alone on the puzzles. The only real difference was the feeling that being told they were working together might create.[11]

The effects of this small manipulation were profound: participants in the *psychologically together* category worked 48 percent longer, solved more problems correctly, and had better recall for what they had seen. They also said that they felt less tired and depleted by the task. They also reported finding the puzzle more interesting when working *together*, and persisted longer because of this *intrinsic* motivation (rather than out of a sense of obligation to the team, which would be an extrinsic motivation).

The word "together" is a powerful social cue to the brain. In and of itself, it seems to serve as a kind of relatedness reward, signaling that you belong, that you are connected, and that there are people you can trust working with you toward the same goal.

Highlight Shared Goals

As it turns out, creating shared goals is one of the most powerful ways to create a sense of in-group among people, no matter what other groups they happen to belong to. That's because the brain is particularly sensitive to whether or not other individuals share a clear goal with you, and when your success depends on theirs. Thus, you can try beginning your request for support by explicitly calling out a goal you share.

For example:

> "Sanjay, I know that your team is also working on ways to expand our client base. I've got a project going on now with the same outcome in mind, and I could really use your expertise. Would you be willing to lend a hand?"

> "Maria, I feel like you and I are both really concerned with the way _____ program is running. And I know you are as committed to success here as I am. I could really use your help with something that I think will significantly improve the program. Could you help me?"

You can use the same principle to foster helpfulness among your whole team or organization. It's one of the reasons people enjoy going after clear, ambitious goals. When everyone knows the goal is to increase sales by 20 percent, or launch some new product by September 1, or invent a widget that can go where no other widget has gone before, they pull together. They help each other.

Find a Common (Out-Group) Enemy

Nothing brings people together quite like mutual dislike for a third party. And just as highlighting shared goals can be a way to make your in-group status salient, so too can reminding someone of the common enemy or competitor you are working against. This is (or, at least, appears to be) a particularly favorite strategy among political campaign operatives. If memory serves, I saw relatively few ads during the run-up to the 2016 US presidential election that actually focused on the merits of either candidate. Instead, they focused largely on why, if elected, the opposing party's candidate would place the United States in a handbasket headed straight to hell. Creating a strong sense of in-group by highlighting a shared threat or nemesis is, perhaps unfortunately, a highly effective way of mobilizing people to action. And you can use this strategy, too, in your day-to-day requests for support.

For example:

> "Zana, I'm working on something that I think will strike a real blow to our main competitor, Company X. Can I ask you to take a look and perhaps lend me some of your expertise?"

> "James, I know that neither one of us really wants to see Stephen promoted to head of sales. I'm

going to throw my hat into the ring on this one. Can I count on your support?"

Again, you can use this technique as a manager, too. But it's a tricky one if you don't want to foster factionalism in your organization. You're better off making the enemy a rival company than a rival business unit.

Talk about Shared Experiences and Feelings, Not Shared Objective Traits

Highlighting things you have in common is another powerful way to create a salient sense of in-group with the person you're seeking help from. But what you have in common (and how you talk about it) turns out to really matter. There are two types of commonalities that psychologists have studied. The first happens when you focus on the *experiences* you have in common—your subjective *feelings* and perceptions about a particular situation, experience, or subject. For example, "Have you ever looked at the city skyline and just been amazed by its beauty? I feel that all the time." Or, "We both know what it's like to feel like our voices aren't heard on this team."

The other, in contrast, is focusing on the objective traits you have in common—that you have the same alma mater, hobby, or hair color. "I went to Harvard;

you did too, right?" or "I just realized that we are both into white-water rafting!"

The two sometimes do go together. For example, if there are only two women on a senior management team, that's a shared objective trait. They may have nothing else in common. But then again, they might. One might create a bond with the other by saying, "We're the only two women on the team. Have you noticed that we get interrupted all the time?" That's a shared trait followed by a shared experience.

But, generally, the power to create a really strong sense of in-group lies in finding common perceptions, thoughts, and feelings, not shared traits. Even though people are biased toward their own groups. Studies show that talking about shared experiences increases our liking for strangers. It makes people feel more connected and serves to validate their view of the world because it is shared.

This is why the best team-building experiences aren't filled with corny "two truths and a lie" getting-to-know-you games. They're focused on building shared experiences and shared sentiments. Like a sense of mutual glee at riding a roller coaster together or a sense of mutual horror at having to sing karaoke in front of a crowd (I actually love karaoke, but I recognize I might be in the minority).

When trying to use thoughtful in-group reinforcement to foster a sense of helpfulness, begin with shared feelings and experiences. You want to create the sense that you are fellow travelers on the same journey.

It Helps to Remember

- Understanding group membership, and when and why we see other people as members of our group (or not), is essential because it is one of the single best predictors of who is—and is not—likely to help you.

- A sense of being in the same group as another person reinforces our desire to help them. This preference for our own group can lead to all sorts of unfairness and bias in supposedly meritocratic systems. But once you understand how the psychology of groups works, you can counteract the unfair aspects.

- We can choose to emphasize the categories we want—like being on the same team, or working together toward the same goal—and make the brain switch to using *that* as the basis for concluding who is in and who is out of our group.

Chapter 8

The Positive Identity Reinforcement

W*hich character from* Game of Thrones *are you? Which Hogwarts house would you belong to? Are you an introvert or an extrovert? An optimist or a realist? Take this Facebook quiz . . .*

People love to learn about themselves, as evidenced by the wild popularity of personality tests. On the surface, this might seem like an exercise in pure egotism, about as productive as gazing into a mirror for hours on end. But as the science shows, trying to really understand yourself fully and accurately—by examining your own thoughts, feelings, and behaviors—is one of the most practically useful things you can ever do.

Most people see themselves (rightly or wrongly) as helpful, because being helpful is part of what it means to be a good person. So helpfulness is generally an important aspect of a typical person's identity. In addition, being a helpful person is a particularly potent way to boost self-esteem, at least in theory. There are, of course, rules and limits involved. So using the potential for positive identity as a reinforcement, just like in-group reinforcement, requires an understanding of how it works.

Know Thyself

Two aspects of your own self-knowledge dramatically influence you (whether or not you realize it). The first is your *identity*, or self-concept. In other words, what you *think* you are like—your traits, your strengths and weaknesses, your attitudes and preferences. You use this knowledge, largely unconsciously, to make hundreds of choices every day. Will you put your hat in the ring for that promotion? What will you do on your next day off? What will you eat for breakfast? Are you going to start watching *Stranger Things*? Your sense of your own identity guides all of these decisions. So knowing what you are like—and being accurate about it—is pretty important. It allows you to choose the best path for you, the one that leads to maximum happiness and success, because it fits you.

Self-knowledge comes from two primary sources. The first is self-perception—quite literally, observing yourself just as you would others. You draw conclusions about yourself and your skills, abilities, and character traits by taking note of your own thoughts and actions. You might assume this would naturally lead to a highly accurate assessment. After all, who knows what you think, feel, and do better than *you* do?

Unfortunately, self-perception is a tricky thing. Because so much of what drives our behavior isn't fully conscious, we aren't always aware of everything going on in our own brains. So we only have, at best, a partial view of the "why" behind what we do. In addition, human memory is an imperfect thing. What we can remember—and how easily—can make a big impact on the conclusions we draw about ourselves.

Imagine that I asked you to recall six instances when you behaved assertively. That's probably not that hard for you to do, right? Maybe last week you spoke up in a meeting to challenge a colleague's point of view. And then the other day, you sent your steak back because the chef had undercooked it. *This is easy*, you think. *I must be pretty assertive.*

Now imagine that instead of asking for six instances, I asked for twelve. A bit more challenging, no? After seven or eight, you start running out of memories, straining to come up with more examples. No surprise, then, that people who are asked to think of six times that they were assertive rate themselves as significantly *more* assertive than those who are asked for twelve.[1] Because no matter how assertive you are, coming up with a dozen specific instances when you behaved that way is hard. And people say to themselves, *if I really was assertive, I should be able to come up with twelve times . . . so I guess I must not be.*

Of course, the other way we know ourselves is through the eyes of others. Our earliest sense of self comes pretty much directly from our childhood caregivers. *If Mommy thinks I'm smart or funny, then I must be.* As we age, we look to our peers and relationship partners, our colleagues and acquaintances, to gather information about what we are like.

Judge Thyself

The second aspect of self-knowledge that shapes your world is how you *feel* about your identity. Do you, generally speaking, like you? Do you think you have mostly good qualities, or bad? A lot of ability, or very little? These evaluations contribute to your *self-esteem*.

Self-esteem is something like an internal identity thermometer. It moves up and down as you get feedback from the world around you about yourself—going up with successes and compliments, and down with setbacks and criticism. But for most of us, these are not wild fluctuations. Much like Oslo or Mexico City, the temperature stays within a certain range. People with high self-esteem tend to not dip down that much, and people with low self-esteem don't enjoy a reprieve from hating themselves for too long.

Self-esteem matters because it provides you with a key piece of information—*How am I doing?* Do I have what it takes to navigate the world—personally, socially, professionally—in such a way that I can reach my goals? High self-esteem says, "Yes. Yes, you can." Consequently, it gives you the confidence and resilience to push through the rough times. Research shows that people with high self-esteem experience more positive and less negative emotions overall. They engage in more effective coping strategies and persist longer when things go wrong. They have greater psychological protection from debilitating life events, like the loss of a job, relationship, or loved one. And they enjoy superior health outcomes across the board, including faster recovery from illness or surgery.

Understanding the importance of these two aspects of self-knowledge—having an accurate view of who you are, and liking who you are—psychologists eventually turned to the next logical question: Which is *more* important? Do people prioritize being right about themselves or thinking highly of themselves?

Evidence suggests that, despite the many twists and contortions people seem to go through to see themselves in a positive light (more on that in a moment), *knowing yourself* is actually the higher priority. People find it so disturbing when they face the possibility that they *don't* know themselves, or have the wrong opinion of themselves, that they react in some highly surprising ways.

Take, for example, a famous study led by psychologist William Swann at the University of Texas at Austin.[2] The researchers invited college student participants into the lab and measured their self-esteem using a questionnaire. Next, they asked them to write a few paragraphs about themselves as part of a personality test that three other college students would evaluate. The researcher later showed the participants the three evaluations (which were fake)—one was positive, one was negative, and one was relatively neutral. Finally, the researcher asked the participants to rate how much they would like to meet each of their reviewers.

Now you might be thinking that everyone would want to meet the person who reviewed them favorably, and you'd be mostly right. But as Swann's research showed, that's because most people view *themselves* favorably. Among those participants who had negative self-views, however, the preference was overwhelmingly for the *negative* reviewer.

When studies like these were first published, many psychologists were skeptical. For years, accepted wisdom was that pretty much everyone would want to interact with other people who would lift their self-esteem, especially those who were a bit down in the dumps about themselves. But it's since become clear that the desire to see oneself positively, while strong, is secondary to the desire to see oneself accurately. If I think I am pretty lousy, then anyone who thinks differently has the potential to cause me great unease. Their views undermine the legitimacy of my own. No thank-you.

You may have seen this phenomenon in action in yourself. Have you ever given a friend or romantic partner a sincere compliment, only to watch them visibly recoil? Or even argue with you?

You: *You're a terrific cook, Susan.*

Susan: *No, I'm actually a terrible cook. You're wrong. My food could literally kill people.*

In the moment, it can feel inexplicable, ungrateful, even hurtful. But such is the intensity of the drive to know yourself accurately. If Susan sees herself as an awful cook—if that's the story she's been telling herself about herself—your compliment might threaten her in ways even she doesn't fully understand. And people who feel threatened, even implicitly, behave badly.

Really, Though, I'm Pretty Great

That said, the vast majority of us do enjoy compliments, because we have largely positive opinions of ourselves. So there is no contradiction. This may surprise you, in so far as you have actually *met* other people and have often found them to be terrible. How do we manage to see ourselves so favorably, despite our many flaws? Well, we humans have no shortage of clever ways to accomplish this trick.

There but for the Grace of God . . .

First, we engage in something called downward social comparison, or, as you may have heard it expressed, "Hey, at least I'm not that guy." These are the C students who compare themselves to the F students, rather than the A students. The person in an unhappy marriage who focuses on the turmoil of her friend's divorce, and the divorcee who is grateful to no longer be among the unhappily married. We compare ourselves to one another constantly—often not entirely consciously—and those comparisons aren't random. They are targeted, often with the aim of finding some poor fool who is worse off, to make us feel better.

Explain Yourself

Do me a favor. Take a quick moment to think about the last time you had a win—a time when you felt successful. (I'll wait.) OK, now, *why* do you think you were successful?

Next, take a moment to think about your last setback. A time when you felt a bit like a failure. Got it? Why do you think you had that setback?

Now, notice anything different about *how* you explained your success and failure? If you are like most people with relatively high self-esteem, you probably explained your success in terms of your skills and abilities, but explained your failure as being the result of the circumstances. *I scored that big account because of my persistence and creative thinking. I lost that big account because my boss has put too much on my plate for me to give them the time they need.*

Psychologists call this a difference in attribution or explanatory style, and what we attribute our wins and losses to turns out to be intimately related to our sense of self-esteem. It's also a critical factor in predicting who experiences helplessness and depression. People with the *optimistic explanatory style* that leads to higher self-esteem and greater resilience tend to attribute their successes to something about themselves that is internal and stable—for example, their intelligence, creativity, work ethic, and so on. In contrast, they attribute their failures to something that is changeable and circumstantial, saying things like: *I didn't get the support I needed, I didn't apply the right strategy, People are working against me.* (OK, that last one is perhaps more paranoid than anything else, but you get the idea.)

Run Away!

Never underestimate the human capacity for denial. One of the most common—and in the short term, reasonably effective—strategies for maintaining high self-esteem is to simply choose to ignore the bad stuff. Most of us have lots of places we can choose to put our attention, so we can, when necessary, choose to put it somewhere other than on our failures and shortcomings. (For example, I can and do avoid my reflection like the plague on days when I'm sleep-deprived and know I look like I've been run over by a truck.) This strategy involves some risk, however, because these things tend to catch up to you. Deny to yourself that you are disorganized or bad with time and you stand little hope of improving on either score. Deny to yourself that you can't see well at night when driving, and you may end up wrapped around a tree.

A close cousin of denial is another ultimately ineffective strategy called "self-handicapping." In essence, the idea is to sabotage your own performance deliberately, so that when you fail, you can blame it on the sabotage rather than something about you—something about your ability or character. Students sometimes self-handicap by deliberately not studying for difficult exams. Romantic partners may engage in distancing or other damaging behaviors that undermine the relationship. In both cases, when things fail—and they will— the failure can be blamed on the lack of study, or the distancing. Both are ultimately less of a blow to one's self-esteem than allowing for the possibility that *I'm not good enough*.

No, but Seriously, I'm Pretty Great

Just as we can choose to ignore our setbacks and weaknesses, so too can we choose to focus our attention like a laser on our best and brightest qualities. We can revel in our own awesomeness, brag to friends and coworkers, and engage in positive self-talk in our bathroom mirrors. Studies show that something as simple as taking a moment to think about our values, like honesty, compassion, generosity, can result in tangible boosts to self-esteem.

Which brings us back, finally, to the topic of this book.

What Helping You Says about Me

People do kind and generous things all the time, often because the situation pretty much calls for it. If you see someone struggling with the door, you hold it open for them. If someone drops their papers in front of you, you stop to help pick them up. You do this with barely a thought, because the norms of society dictate that, much like driving on a particular side of the road or not urinating in public, *this is what you do* if you want to live among us. When we behave in a helpful manner, we don't necessarily get a reinforcement unless that behavior is explicitly connected to our identity. In other words, it's not that I did something helpful; it's that I am *a helpful person*. The latter is where the reinforcement—and consequently the added motivation and benefits to well-being—lies.

Studies show, for example, that in children as young as three, being told that they could "be a helper" was more motivating and led to more effort than simply "helping" in tasks like assisting another child in cleaning up blocks.

Similarly, people are reliably more likely to vote if you ask them, "How important is it to you to *be a voter?*" the day before an election than, "How important is it to you to vote?"[3] And people make bigger contributions to charity when asked if they would like to be a "generous donor" than they do if they are simply asked to donate.

Making a direct connection to how helpfulness relates to the kind of person you are is also essential for tapping into a very powerful source of positive identity reinforcement: gratitude. You read a lot these days about research showing that practicing gratitude—making a deliberate point of *being* grateful for the good things in your life—has all sorts of benefits for happiness and well-being. These articles usually end with a call to the reader to start keeping a gratitude journal to reap the full personal benefits of being thankful.

There's nothing wrong with that. But it's also worthwhile to keep in mind gratitude's other, arguably even more important purpose: to strengthen our relationships with those upon whom we rely and make them more likely to support us again in the future.

Historically, most of the research on gratitude has focused on its social function, not its impact on our own brains. This body of research has found, to put it bluntly, that expressing gratitude to someone who helps you keeps them interested and invested in having a relationship with you over the long haul. It makes their time, effort, and inconvenience seem worth it.

In the same vein, there is nothing quite like *in*gratitude to sour an otherwise happy relationship. Most of us can recall a time when we were shocked at how unappreciative and thoughtless someone was in response to our generosity. (And if you are a parent, chances are you just have to think back to this morning's breakfast.) Without some sort of acknowledgment, people very quickly stop wanting to help you. In a set of studies by Francesca Gino and Adam Grant, the absence of thanks for previous help given saw future helping rates cut immediately in half.[4]

Gratitude is a glue that binds you and your benefactor together, allowing you to hit the same well over and over again when you need support, knowing that it won't run dry.

The critical thing to remember when providing positive identity reinforcement is to put the emphasis—either in your initial request, or in your subsequent expression of thanks—on the *kind of person* the helper is, and how providing you with support is an expression of *who they are*. Remember what we covered in chapter 6: saying thank-you the right way means praising the other person for being kind, generous, selfless, and good-looking. (OK, maybe not the last one.) It does not mean talking about how their help let you enjoy a hard-earned vacation or helped you impress the boss. You may be the one who needs help, but if you want it to be motivating and rewarding, it needs to be all about them.

The Helper's Identity Matters, Not Yours

On that note, remember that what would give *you* a positive identity boost isn't, necessarily, what will do it for them. Asking me to donate to the Humane Society so I can be a "friend to all animals" really only works if I want to be friend to all animals. Maybe I hate animals. In which case, asking me to donate so I can help get stray animals in shelters and be a "defender of our community" against the scourge of wild dogs is going to be a much better pitch.

Often, the same exact behavior we're trying to solicit for support can be framed as serving multiple purposes and thus enhancing different positive identities. The key is finding the right one.

For example, studies suggest that pro-environment messages are often framed exclusively in relatively narrow moral terms that appeal specifically to liberal values, evoking concepts like *injustice, harm*, or *care*.[5] Consequently, these messages are motivating only to liberals, for whom they hold the potential to create positive identity. However, when researchers frame these same messages in moral terms that appeal to conservatives, including concepts like *purity* and *sanctity, respect for authority*, and *patriotism*, a different pattern emerges:

Liberal appeal:
Show your love for all of humanity and the world in which we live by helping to care for our vulnerable natural environment. Help to reduce the harm done to the environment by taking action. By caring for the natural world you are helping to ensure that everyone around the world gets to enjoy fair access to a sustainable environment. Do the right thing by preventing the suffering of all life forms and making sure that no one is denied their right to a healthy planet. Show your compassion!

Conservative appeal:
Show you love your country by joining the fight to protect the purity of America's natural environment. Take pride in the American tradition of performing one's civic duty by taking responsibility for yourself and the land you call home. By taking a tougher stance on protecting the natural environment, you will be honoring all of Creation. Demonstrate your respect by following the examples of your religious and political leaders

who defend America's natural environment.
Show your patriotism!

Researchers found that when pro-environment messages matched the political and moral values of participants, they emerged with greater intentions to engage in
pro-environment behaviors and stronger endorsement
of the danger of climate change.[6] So to maximize positive identity reinforcement, know your audience and
emphasize what matters to them, not to you.

Obi-Wan Kenobi, You're My Only Hope

In a previous chapter, we talked about the importance of
avoiding *diffusion of responsibility* when making requests
for support. Sending an email to fifty people asking for
the same favor makes it all too easy for any one of them
to say, "I don't need to do this. Someone else will."

But there is another critical insight about helper motivation that is often overlooked here: the very fact that
someone else *could* help you undermines the potential
positive identity reinforcement for me. Because what
people really want to give is unique or, to use the technical term, "nonsubstitutable" help. Help that only *they*
can give. Because the more unique the help, the more
closely tied it is to who they are.

Studies show that giving that involves your "essence"—your name (in the form of your signature), your personal possessions, or physical body (e.g., blood donation)—increases self-perceptions of generosity and commitment to ongoing support, compared to other gifts of equal value, like money. Being asked to give of the "self" has also been linked to greater generosity when people are given a future opportunity to help.[7]

For instance, in one study, researchers gave participants pens and then asked them on their way out of the study to donate the pen to children in developing countries. Those who had been given the pen at the beginning of the study rated themselves more generous and committed than those given it at the end, because enough time had passed to make it feel as if the pen was really their possession.

In a second study, people who purchased cookies to support a charity and wrote their name on the order felt more generous and committed than those who simply paid for the cookie.

There are really two things going on here. The first is that giving of the self—giving something only you can give—results in an increased subjective value of the donation. Because one of the most robust findings in all of psychology is something called the *endowment effect*, namely, that we all think that our own stuff is worth more just because it's *ours*. (A quick example from a typical experiment: an undergraduate walks into the lab. You show them a really nice mug with their university insignia on it and ask them how much of their own money they'd be willing to spend to buy it. They say, "Three dollars." A second undergraduate walks into the lab. You *give* them the really nice mug. And now you ask them how much you have to pay them to get it back. They say, "Five dollars." Because now that they *own* the mug, it just seems more valuable. And this, in essence, is why every real estate transaction is pretty much a total nightmare.)

The second thing happening is that unique helping provides greater integration of the generous act into one's own self-concept. After all, helping that only I can give must say something pretty great about me.

So to activate the positive identity reinforcement, find ways to convey that the helper is in a unique position to help you—that they, like Obi-Wan, are really your only hope.

It Helps to Remember

- People have a strong need to see themselves as good people. A positive sense of identity is a powerful reinforcer of behavior.

- When confronted with evidence that we're *not* good people, most of us will discount it. Conversely, when we have an opportunity to see ourselves as being good people, rather than just people who occasionally do good things, we will seize it.

- Studies show, for example, that for children as young as three, being told that they could "be a helper" was more motivating and led to more effort than simply "helping" in tasks like assisting another child in cleaning up blocks.

- When providing positive identity reinforcement, put the emphasis—either in your initial request or in your subsequent expression of thanks—on the kind of person the helper is and how providing you with support expresses who they are.

Chapter 9

The Effectiveness Reinforcement

W*hat is the meaning of life?*
        OK, wait, I don't want to tackle that one. Let me tone it down a little . . .

What do people want?

Still a pretty big question—one that psychologists have argued about for as long as psychology has been a thing. Before that, it was the philosophers who wrestled with it. And, of course, neither group owns the market on the subject. Sociologists, political scientists (and politicians), military leaders, marketing executives, educators, lobbyists, activists, and influencers of all shapes and sizes are all in the business of trying to figure out what motivates people to do what they do.

If you randomly ask someone on the street this question, the answer you will get is probably going to be some form of "people want to be happy." Founding father of psychology and cigar enthusiast Sigmund Freud would give an answer—which formed the implicit basis for how psychologists approached motivation for a century—along the same lines. He said that human beings wanted to approach pleasure and avoid pain. Period. Full stop. If something feels good (or gets us a feel-good reward), we do it. If it hurts, we don't.

On the face of it, this feels obviously true. So the scientific community, and the public at large, pretty much bought into it. Hence, a hundred years of trying to motivate people by finding ever more effective carrots and sticks.

Only . . . it's wrong. Or perhaps more accurately, it's a deeply flawed account of why human beings do things. Because there is something even more important than pleasure and pain, and if you want to make sure other people actually benefit from helping you, you need to know what it is.

You see, the problem with the approach pleasure/avoid pain account of human motivation is pretty obvious when you think about. People forgo pleasure and even approach pain, all the time. Think of:

- The marathon runner, training for endless hours every day in deliberately difficult conditions. (And don't give me that runner's high nonsense. There is no high that makes that amount of running literally *feel good*.)

- The parents who endure sleep deprivation and constant anxiety to care for their children. (Especially that second or third child, because at that point, you know what you're getting yourself into.)

- The students who study all day, every day— subjects like organic chemistry and advanced calculus—for a shot at a medical school program. (That they know full well will torture them for four more years, after which they encounter the hellscape of residency.)

- The soldiers who knowingly put their lives at risk to save their comrades or to protect innocent civilians.

We need not even get that dramatic about it. Think of *you*. Think of what you did today. (Or, if you are reading this during breakfast, think of yesterday.) What percentage of your day was devoted to things you found pleasure in doing—things for which there was an immediate reward? OK, now think of how much you did that was hard, stressful, tedious, or otherwise unpleasant. Can you honestly say that "approach pleasure and avoid pain" is the guiding principle of *your* life?

Not mine, either. Not any of us. The very fact that people are, with remarkable frequency, willing to die for what they believe in and for the things that matter to them means this *can't* be what life is about. Because the pleasure is over at that point.

Everybody may want to be happy, but happiness isn't the motivating force behind most of what human beings do. It isn't what keeps us going. It is, surprisingly, not much of a reinforcer. So you don't really need to worry about whether or not your request for help will actually make the helper happy—whether the actual *act* of helping will be fun, exciting, or otherwise pleasurable. And that's good news, because most helping is hard work.

So far, I've talked about two helping reinforcers—a sense of *in-group* and *positive identity*. Technically, you don't need both to be present when making a request for help; either one will do the trick. There is, however, one reinforcer that really *must* be present if your helper is going to reap the well-being rewards of helping. Simply put, it's the opportunity for them to feel *effective*.

It's All about Impact

No psychologist since B. F. Skinner has probably done more to shape the science of motivation than E. Tory Higgins. (Full disclosure: Higgins was my mentor and a coauthor of one of my books. But I'm telling you, the guy is the real deal.)

In one of his recent books, *Beyond Pleasure and Pain*, Higgins argued that the desire to feel effective—to know what's real, manage what happens, and achieve the outcome you're looking for—is what truly engages people and gives their lives meaning. We want to affect the world around us, to have an impact, even if only a small one. Happiness is frankly beside the point. People routinely choose to live lives of suffering and self-sacrifice because it's the *impact* of their choices that matters most.

Entrepreneurs aren't "happy" putting in hundred-hour workweeks to get their startups off the ground. Olympic-level athletes don't find it "fun" to give up having normal, friend-filled lives to single-mindedly pursue excellence in their sport. There is nothing like "pleasure" in the sleep deprivation required to feed and care for a newborn infant, night after night. But there *is* impact. There is—or at least there can be—a feeling of effectiveness that can keep us going and going and going.

What happens when people lack a feeling of effectiveness? In the short term, it wipes out motivation entirely. Research shows that when people are unable to get any kind of feedback about how well they are doing on a task, they quickly become disengaged from it.[1] This has everything to do with how the motivational systems in the brain are wired. You expend effort and initiate actions only when your brain detects a discrepancy between the goal state you are trying to reach and where you currently are with respect to the goal. (This is why, for example, weighing yourself regularly when dieting is important. Knowing how much you have left to lose is a big part of what keeps you going. So, too, does the sense that you are closing the gap and making progress—in other words, that what you're doing is effective.)

In the long term, a lack of feeling effective is associated with clinical levels of helplessness and depression. Research suggests that one of the hallmarks of depressive thinking is the tendency to attribute the negative outcomes in your life to factors that are both outside your own control and relatively stable.[2] (*My relationships don't work out because I'm unlovable. I'm not getting promoted at work because I'm just not talented. I didn't get a raise because my manager has it in for me.*) Failing to have the impact you are seeking in your life, again and again, can create the sense that you are powerless to effect real change.

When you can't shake the feeling of ineffectiveness, lack of motivation becomes something far worse: a lack of purpose and meaning. Consider a person who works on a product launch day in, day out for several months. The product launches and starts bringing in a modest amount of revenue. It's not as much as the person was expecting, but neither is it a complete disaster. To discuss next steps, she schedules an after-action review with the team and the executives who asked for her help on the project. One of the executives brushes aside the revenue the new product is earning as totally insignificant. Even worse, the other executive admits that he *completely forgot* he'd asked her to work on the project at all. She leaves feeling completely demotivated. Not only is the product she worked on ineffective, but the entire assignment was so trivial that one of the executive sponsors forgot about its existence.

Not surprisingly then, the desire to feel effective when it comes to helping—to really see your helping efforts *land*—is critical for sustaining the motivation to help and for reaping the psychological rewards of helping. If I work nights and weekends to launch a product that you've completely forgotten about, will I be excited about doing any project you assign to me in the future? If I donate money to your cause without a clear sense of the tangible impact my money is having on the lives of others, what gratification can I really derive from it? If I write you a letter of recommendation for a new job and never hear from you again, how am I supposed to feel about the trouble I went through on your behalf? How do I know it was worth it? Moreover, how do I know that my time, money, or effort wouldn't be *better* spent some other way?

Seeing Your Help Land Means More (and More Rewarding) Helping

Research has made it clear that the effectiveness of helping is an essential reinforcer. For example, take a study that asked participants to donate to one of two different charities: UNICEF and Spread the Net.[3] The UNICEF appeal was relatively general and abstract, because UNICEF is a large organization that funds a variety of children's health-care initiatives. While a donation to UNICEF would clearly benefit children in need, it was unclear to donors exactly who would benefit and how. The Spread the Net appeal, in contrast, was more concrete and descriptive. It explained that it would use the funds to buy bed nets to stop the spread of malaria in regions of the world where it was endemic. Researchers found that larger donations to charity predicted larger increases in well-being, but *only* for those donors who gave to Spread the Net (not UNICEF) and consequently could clearly understand the impact of their helping.

Effectiveness doesn't just have an impact on the psychological benefits of helping; it has an impact on the likelihood you will help in the first place. For example, putting yourself in the shoes of a person in need—and experiencing empathy as a result—is more likely to lead to increased helping when people believe they will receive some kind of feedback about the support they gave.[4] In addition, many researchers argue that the reason identifiable victims consistently receive more assistance than anonymous ones is because potential helpers can more easily imagine the difference their efforts will make.[5]

Research by Adam Grant, Francesca Gino, and others has shown that feelings of effectiveness also directly influence the likelihood of providing continuing support over time.[6] In one study, for example, students who received a thank-you note from a help recipient were more willing to offer additional help to them, and even to others.[7] Gratitude is, of course, a factor here, but at least as important is knowing that the help you gave made a difference.

In another study, volunteers who raised funds for a university scholarship were given different levels of exposure to their beneficiaries. Some had no contact, others read a letter from a past scholarship recipient, and a third group had the opportunity to meet and briefly interact with a recipient, who spoke of how the scholarship had changed their lives.

One month later, researchers found that direct interpersonal contact with a beneficiary of helping had more than doubled the number of minutes volunteers spent on the phone soliciting donations and the total donation solicited. Follow-up studies showed that these effects were obtained because meeting the beneficiary of their hard work increased the perception of its impact and importance. Interestingly, simply reading the letter was not enough to have an impact on rates of helping.

In yet another study, Grant studied the productivity of new employees at the outbound call center in a privately held company in the Midwest that sold educational and marketing software to institutions of higher education and nonprofits.[8] The revenue that these workers created supported jobs in another department, but they had no direct contact with these people.

Grant asked one beneficiary from the other department to speak at the call center for ten minutes about how the revenue they generated supported job creation and made his own job possible. He found that this brief but powerful intervention had dramatic results, nearly doubling call-center sales and revenue in subsequent months.

Making efforts on others' behalf can, of course, be draining, particularly given the number of responsibilities and stresses each of us is juggling. Helping can involve more than just work—for example, when the person in need is distraught or down, helping may involve psychologically taxing tasks like taking perspectives, regulating emotions, and working through complex problems. But research shows that knowing that the help you gave had an impact can go a long way to refilling your tank.[9]

In one study, researchers asked MBA students to complete a daily survey for fifteen consecutive workdays. They measured helping with questions like "Today, I went out of my way to help coworkers who asked for my help with work-related problems." They measured feelings of effectiveness and impact with items like "I feel that my help with the above issues made a positive difference in coworkers' lives today." Researchers found that the MBA students' daily sense of depletion and fatigue was directly related to the impact of their helping—the *more* impact they had, the *less* drained they felt.

How You Can Increase Your Helpers' Sense of Effectiveness

That helpers need to feel effective in order to want to support you, to benefit from supporting you, and to sustain that support over time is perhaps the most overlooked factor when it comes to soliciting help. Here are some things you can do to make sure your helpers will know that their help got the job done:

1. **Be clear up-front about the nature of assistance you want and what its impact will be.** Vague, indirect appeals make it difficult for people to imagine how it's all going to work and whether or not they

will have an impact. I have frequently received requests, for example, from people who wanted to "get together over coffee" and "pick my brain about some things." I say no to these requests literally every time. When I have no idea what you want, or why, or how *exactly* I might be of help to you, I'm not interested. No one is.

2. Follow up afterward. Let them know in advance that you will. It doesn't feel good to wonder if the time and effort you put into something was worth it. It doesn't feel good to wonder if the person in need ended up better off or worse. Take the time to let people know the impact they had on you and how things turned out. Letting someone know at the time of the request that you intend to follow up gives them that much more confidence that they will end up feeling effective.

3. Allow people to choose how they help you, if possible. Be direct and specific about the kind of help you are looking for. But just as important, be willing to accept alternative offers of help, even if it isn't what you originally wanted. People will often want some flexibility. After all, helpers want to give the help that is most likely to be effective, something they can actually do, given all the other demands on their time. The other day, a

reporter wanted to schedule a call with me for a story on first impressions. The timeline was tight, and I was booked solid with meetings for the next two days. So I offered to answer the questions via email instead, knowing that while not ideal, at least I would be able to help in some way. The reporter ended up with a few usable quotes and was able to turn in the story on time. I ended up feeling good about the help I could give, instead of having to just say no.

Thinking about the effectiveness reinforcement helped me finally understand a classic children's book by Shel Silverstein: *The Giving Tree*. I had never really understood that book's appeal. Here's a short summary if you have not read it: tree and boy love each other. Over the years, the boy increasingly ignores and neglects the tree, though he does stop by on occasion to ask the tree for her apples, branches, trunk, and so on for his own seemingly selfish reasons, which the tree willingly agrees to give him out of love. In the end, when all that is left of her is a stump, the boy—now an old man—returns to sit on her. At which point—and I'm quoting here—"The tree was happy." To say the tree gets the short end of the stick here is the understatement of the century.

But seen through the lens of effectiveness, the tree's happiness makes sense: the tree is pretty darn effective at giving the boy what he asks for. (I still think the boy is awfully selfish, though.)

As a colleague and as a manager of people, helping people see the impact of their work—their help—is one of the most important motivators you can wield.

We're All in This Together

I'll be totally honest. I've never been good at asking for help. Or, rather, all my life I've avoided doing it like the plague. In high school, I refused to ask my mother, *who is German*, for help on my very challenging German translation assignments. I spent hours in college pouring over library books just to avoid asking the teaching assistant for the answer to a question that would have taken him five minutes to provide. I put myself deeply in debt in graduate school, rather than asking my parents for more support, because I was embarrassed to admit I couldn't make ends meet. I clean my house *before* the housekeeper gets here, so she doesn't have to deal with my mess. The list goes on and on.

Writing this book has been eye-opening for me, because it's forced me to realize that my discomfort about seeking help stems from precisely the same mistakes I've been telling you not to make. I've been terrified someone will say no. I've assumed people will think less of me for needing help. And worse, I've believed deep down that having to help is awful, and I have no right to ask it of anyone.

None of that is true. Not one bit of it. The evidence couldn't be clearer.

People are helpful much more often than not. People don't think less of you for needing help. And helping, with the right reinforcers in place, feels wonderful. There is no better way to give someone the opportunity to feel good about themselves than to ask them to help you. It brings out the best—and the best feelings—in all of us.

So let's take the lessons from this book and start living them together. I will do it if you will. And when our time of need arises, let's not hesitate to call for reinforcements.

It Helps to Remember

- Effectiveness is the third major reinforcement that help seekers need to keep in mind. Simply put, people want to know that they've made a difference.

- Conversely, when people have a sense that their work doesn't make any difference, they lose motivation. In the long term, a lack of feeling effective is associated with clinical levels of helplessness and depression.

- The desire to feel effective when it comes to helping—to really see your helping efforts land—is an essential reinforcement both for sustaining the motivation to help and for reaping the psychological rewards of helping.

- When you ask for someone's help, make sure you emphasize what the impact will be. And when you thank them for helping—and you will thank them, won't you?—be sure to let them know the results of their efforts.

Notes

Chapter 1

1. Personal communication, January 7, 2017.
2. Michael Luo, "'Excuse Me. May I Have Your Seat?'" *New York Times*, September 14, 2004, http://www.nytimes.com/2004/09/14/nyregion/excuse-me-may-i-have-your-seat.html.
3. Ibid.
4. N. Weinstein and R. M. Ryan, "When Helping Helps: Autonomous Motivation for Prosocial Behavior and Its Influence on Well-Being for the Helper and Recipient," *Journal of Personality and Social Psychology* 98, no. 2 (2010): 222.
5. Matt Lieberman, *Social: Why Our Brains Are Wired to Connect* (New York: Crown Publishers, 2013), 43.
6. David Rock, *Your Brain at Work* (New York: HarperCollins, 2009).
7. K. D. Williams and B. Jarvis, "Cyberball: A Program for Use in Research on Interpersonal Ostracism and Acceptance," *Behavior Research Methods* 38, no. 1 (2006): 174–180.

Chapter 2

1. F. J. Flynn and V. K. Lake, "If You Need Help, Just Ask: Underestimating Compliance with Direct Requests for Help," *Journal of Personality and Social Psychology* 95, no. 1 (2008): 128.
2. Ibid.
3. Ibid.

4. V. K. Bohns, "(Mis)Understanding Our Influence Over Others: A Review of the Underestimation-of-Compliance Effect," *Current Directions in Psychological Science* 25, no. 2 (2016): 119–123.

5. D. A. Newark, F. J. Flynn, and V. K. Bohns, "Once Bitten, Twice Shy: The Effect of a Past Refusal on Expectations of Future Compliance," *Social Psychological and Personality Science* 5, no. 2 (2014): 218–225.

6. Personal communication, January 7, 2017.

7. Flynn, "If You Need Help, Just Ask."

8. Personal communication, January 7, 2017.

9. Ibid.

10. Peter Economy, "Steve Jobs on the Remarkable Power of Asking for Help," *Inc.*, June 11, 2015, http://www.inc.com/peter-economy/steve-jobs-on-the-remarkable-power-of-asking-for-what-you-want.html.

11. R. B. Cialdini, *Influence, Revised Edition* (New York: HarperCollins, 1987).

12. R. B. Cialdini et al., "Reciprocal Concessions Procedure for Inducing Compliance: The Door-in-the-Face Technique," *Journal of Personality and Social Psychology* 31 (1975): 206–215.

Chapter 3

1. Benjamin Franklin and Hanna Amelia (Noyes) Davidson, *Autobiography of Benjamin Franklin: With Selections from His Other Writings* (Boston: DC Heath & Co, 1908).

2. J. Jecker and D. Landy, "Liking a Person as a Function of Doing Him a Favour," *Human Relations* 22, no. 4 (1969): 371–378.

3. M. E. McCullough, R. A. Emmons, and J. A. Tsang, "The Grateful Disposition: A Conceptual and Empirical Topography," *Journal of Personality and Social Psychology* 82, no. 1 (2002): 112.

4. F. Martela and R. M. Ryan, "The Benefits of Benevolence: Basic Psychological Needs, Beneficence, and the Enhancement of Well-Being," *Journal of Personality* 84, no. 6 (2016): 750–764.

5. J. G. Holland, *The Life of Abraham Lincoln* (Springfield, MA: Gurdon Bill, 1866), 78–79.

6. R. B. Cialdini, B. L. Darby, and J. E. Vincent, "Transgression and Altruism: A Case for Hedonism," *Journal of Experimental Social Psychology* 9, no. 6 (1973): 502–516.

7. M. Estrada-I-Iollenbeck and T. F. Heatherton, "Avoiding and Alleviating Guilt through Prosocial Behavior," in J. Bybee, *Guilt and Children* (Amsterdam: Elsevier, 1997), 215.

8. J. F. Helliwell and R. D. Putnam, "The Social Context of Well-Being," *Philosophical Transactions of the Royal Society B: Biological Sciences* 359, no. 1449 (2004): 1435.

9. E. W. Dunn, L. B. Aknin, and M. I. Norton, "Spending Money on Others Promotes Happiness," *Science* 319, no. 5870 (2008): 1687–1688; and C. E. Schwartz, P. M. Keyl, J. P. Marcum, and R. Bode, "Helping Others Shows Differential Benefits on Health and Well-Being for Male and Female Teens," *Journal of Happiness Studies* 10, no. 4 (2009): 431–448.

Chapter 4

1. M. S. Hagger, N. L. Chatzisarantis, T. Culverhouse, and S. J. Biddle, "The Processes by Which Perceived Autonomy Support in Physical Education Promotes Leisure-Time Physical Activity Intentions and Behavior: A Trans-Contextual Model," *Journal of Educational Psychology* 95, no. 4 (2003): 784.

2. G. C. Williams et al., "Motivational Predictors of Weight Loss and Weight-Loss Maintenance," *Journal of Personality and Social Psychology* 70, no. 1 (1996): 115.

3. G. C. Williams, Z. R. Freedman, and E. L. Deci, "Supporting Autonomy to Motivate Patients with Diabetes for Glucose Control," *Diabetes Care* 21, no. 10 (1998): 1644–1651; G. G. Williams, M. Gagné, R. M. Ryan, and E. L. Deci, "Facilitating Autonomous Motivation for Smoking Cessation," *Health Psychology* 21, no. 1 (2002): 40; and R. M. Ryan, R. W. Plant, and S. O'Malley, "Initial Motivations for Alcohol Treatment: Relations

with Patient Characteristics, Treatment Involvement, and Drop-out," *Addictive Behaviors* 20, no. 3 (1995): 279–297.

4. R. J. Vallerand, M. S. Fortier, and F. Guay, "Self-Determination and Persistence in a Real-Life Setting: Toward a Motivational Model of High School Dropout," *Journal of Personality and Social Psychology* 72, no. 5 (1997): 1161.

5. R. M. Ryan, S. Rigby, and K. King, "Two Types of Religious Internalization and Their Relations to Religious Orientations and Mental Health," *Journal of Personality and Social Psychology* 65 (1993): 586.

6. J. Rodin and E. J. Langer, "Long-Term Effects of a Control-Relevant Intervention with the Institutionalized Aged," *Journal of Personality and Social Psychology* 35, no. 12 (1977): 897.

7. D. B. Thoman, J. L. Smith, and P. J. Silvia, "The Resource Replenishment Function of Interest," *Social Psychological and Personality Science* 2, no. 6 (2011): 592–599.

8. M. R. Lepper, D. Greene, and R. E. Nisbett, "Undermining Children's Intrinsic Interest with Extrinsic Reward: A Test of the 'Overjustification' Hypothesis," *Journal of Personality and Social Psychology* 28, no. 1 (1973): 129.

9. V. K. Bohns and F. J. Flynn, "'Why Didn't You Just Ask?' Underestimating the Discomfort of Help-Seeking," *Journal of Experimental Social Psychology* 46, no. 2 (2010): 402–409.

10. A. M. Isen, M. Clark, and F. Schwartz, "Duration of the Effect of Good Mood on Helping: 'Footprints on the Sands of Time'," *Journal of Personality and Social Psychology* 34, no. 3 (1976): 385.

11. F. J. Flynn, "Identity Orientations and Forms of Social Exchange in Organizations," *Academy of Management Review* 30, no. 4 (2005): 737–750.

12. S. C. Lin, R. L. Schaumberg, and T. Reich, "Sidestepping the Rock and the Hard Place: The Private Avoidance of Prosocial Requests," *Journal of Experimental Social Psychology* 64 (2016): 35–40.

Chapter 5

1. C. Korte, I. Ypma, and A. Toppen, "Helpfulness in Dutch Society as a Function of Urbanization and Environmental Input Level," *Journal of Personality and Social Psychology* 32, no. 6 (1975): 996.

2. M. Schaller and R. B. Cialdini, "Happiness, Sadness, and Helping: A Motivational Integration," in E. T. Higgens and R. M. Sorrentino (eds.), *Handbook of Motivation and Cognition: Foundations of Social Behavior,* vol. 2 (New York: Guilford Press, 1990).

3. C. N. DeWall, R. F. Baumeister, N. L. Mead, and K. D. Vohs, "How Leaders Self-Regulate Their Task Performance: Evidence That Power Promotes Diligence, Depletion, and Disdain," *Journal of Personality and Social Psychology* 100, no. 1 (2011): 47.

4. B. Latane, S. A. Nida, and D. W. Wilson, "The Effects of Group Size on Helping Behavior," in J. P. Rushton and R. M. Sorrentino, eds., *Altruism and Helping Behavior: Social Personality and Developmental Perspectives* (Hillside, NJ: Lawrence Erlbaum Associates, 1981), 287–313.

5. B. Latane and J. M. Darley, "Group Inhibition of Bystander Intervention in Emergencies," *Journal of Personality and Social Psychology* 10, no. 3 (1986): 215.

6. R. L. Shotland and M. K. Straw, "Bystander Response to an Assault: When a Man Attacks a Woman," *Journal of Personality and Social Psychology* 34, no. 5 (1976): 990.

7. V. K. Bohns and F. J. Flynn, "'Why Didn't You Just Ask?' Underestimating the Discomfort of Help-Seeking," *Journal of Experimental Social Psychology* 46, no. 2 (2010): 402–409.

8. R. B. Cialdini, "The Science of Persuasion," *Scientific American Mind* 14, no. 1 (2004): 70–77; and D. R. Shaffer, M. Rogle, and C. Hendrick, "Intervention in the Library: The Effect of Increased Responsibility on Bystanders' Willingness to Prevent a Theft," *Journal of Applied Social Psychology* 5, no. 4 (1975): 303–319.

9. S. E. Anderson and L. J. Williams, "Interpersonal, Job, and Individual Factors Related to Helping Processes at Work," *Journal of Applied Psychology* 81, no. 3 (1996): 282.

10. Bureau of Labor Statistics, 2009.

11. R. Manning, M. Levine, and A. Collins, "The Kitty Genovese Murder and the Social Psychology of Helping: The Parable of the 38 Witnesses," *American Psychologist* 62, no. 6 (2007): 555.

12. Martin Gansberg, "37 Who Saw Murder Didn't Call the Police," *New York Times*, March 27, 1964, http://www.nytimes.com/1964/03/27/37-who-saw-murder-didnt-call-the-police.html.

13. Sarah Kaplan, "Winston Moseley, Killer in Kitty Genovese Case That Became a Symbol of Urban Apathy, Dies in Prison at 81," *Washington Post*, April 5, 2016, https://www.washingtonpost.com/news/morning-mix/wp/2016/04/05/winston-moseley-killer-in-kitty-genovese-case-that-became-a-symbol-of-urban-apathy-dies-in-prison-at-81/.

14. J. M. Darley and B. Latane, "Bystander Intervention in Emergencies: Diffusion of Responsibility," *Journal of Personality and Social Psychology* 8, no. 4 (1968): 377.

15. Luke 10:29–37 (Revised Standard Version).

16. J. M. Darley and C. D. Batson, "'From Jerusalem to Jericho': A Study of Situational and Dispositional Variables in Helping Behavior," *Journal of Personality and Social Psychology* 27, no. 1 (1973): 100.

Chapter 6

1. D. C. Feiler, L. P. Tost, and A. M. Grant, "Mixed Reasons, Missed Givings: The Costs of Blending Egoistic and Altruistic Reasons in Donation Requests," *Journal of Experimental Social Psychology* 48, no. 6 (2012): 1322–1328.

2. S. B. Algoe, L. E. Kurtz, and N. M. Hilaire, "Putting the 'You' in 'Thank You': Examining Other-Praising Behavior as the Active Relational Ingredient in Expressed Gratitude," *Social Psychological and Personality Science* 7, no. 7 (2016): 658–666.

Chapter 7

1. K. Lagattuta and D. Weller, "Interrelations between Theory of Mind and Morality," in M. Killen, J. G. Smetana, and J. Smetana (eds.), *Handbook of Moral Development* (London: Psychology Press, 2014), 385–407.

2. H. Bernhard, U. Fischbacher, and E. Fehr, "Parochial Altruism in Humans," *Nature* 442, no. 7105 (2006): 912–915.

3. S. M. Gaddis, "Discrimination in the Credential Society: An Audit Study of Race and College Selectivity in the Labor Market," *Social Forces* 93, no. 4 (2014): 1451–1479.

4. C. L. Martin, "Attitudes and Expectations about Children with Nontraditional and Traditional Gender Roles," *Sex Roles* 22, no. 3–4 (1990): 151–166.

5. J. M. Burkart, S. B. Hrdy, and C. P. Van Schaik, "Cooperative Breeding and Human Cognitive Evolution," *Evolutionary Anthropology: Issues, News, and Reviews* 18, no. 5 (2009), 175–186.

6. H. Tajfel, "Social Psychology of Intergroup Relations," *Annual Review of Psychology* 33, no. 1 (1982): 1–39.

7. A. P. Fiske, "The Four Elementary Forms of Sociality: Framework for a Unified Theory of Social Relations," *Psychological Review* 99, no. 4 (1992): 689.

8. L. M. Hackel, J. Zaki, and J. J. Van Bavel, "Social Identity Shapes Social Valuation: Evidence from Prosocial Behavior and Vicarious Reward," *Social Cognitive and Affective Neuroscience* 12, no. 8 (2017): 1219–1228.

9. D. N. Den Hartog, A. H. De Hoogh, and A. E. Keegan, "The Interactive Effects of Belongingness and Charisma on Helping and Compliance," *Journal of Applied Psychology* 92, no. 4 (2007): 1131.

10. J. J. Van Bavel and W. A. Cunningham, "Self-Categorization with a Novel Mixed-Race Group Moderates Automatic Social and Racial Biases," *Personality and Social Psychology Bulletin* 35, no. 3 (2009): 321–335.

11. P. B. Carr, and G. M. Walton, "Cues of Working Together Fuel Intrinsic Motivation," *Journal of Experimental Social Psychology* 53 (2014): 169–184.

Chapter 8

1. N. Schwarz et al., "Ease of Retrieval as Information: Another Look at the Availability Heuristic," *Journal of Personality and Social Psychology* 61, no. 2 (1991): 195.

2. W. B. Swann et al., "Allure of Negative Feedback: Self-Verification Strivings among Depressed Persons," *Journal of Abnormal Psychology* 101, no. 2 (1992): 293.

3. C. J. Bryan, G. M. Walton, T. Rogers, and C. S. Dweck, "Motivating Voter Turnout by Invoking the Self," *Proceedings of the National Academy of Sciences* 108, no. 31 (2011): 12653–12656.

4. Francesca Gino and Adam Grant, "The Big Benefits of a Little Thanks," *Harvard Business Review*, November 2013, https://hbr.org/2013/11/the-big-benefits-of-a-little-thanks.

5. S. Clayton, A. Koehn, and E. Grover, "Making Sense of the Senseless: Identity, Justice, and the Framing of Environmental Crises," *Social Justice Research* 26, no. 3 (2013): 301–319.

6. C. Wolsko, H. Ariceaga, and J. Seiden, "Red, White, and Blue Enough to Be Green: Effects of Moral Framing on Climate Change Attitudes and Conservation Behaviors," *Journal of Experimental Social Psychology* 65 (2016): 7–19.

7. M. Koo and A. Fishbach, "Giving the Self: Increasing Commitment and Generosity through Giving Something That Represents One's Essence," *Social Psychological and Personality Science* 7, no. 4 (2016): 339–348.

Chapter 9

1. G. Oettingen et al., "Nonconscious Goal Pursuit: Acting in an Explanatory Vacuum," *Journal of Experimental Social Psychology* 42, no. 5 (2006): 668–675.

2. Martin E. Seligman, *Learned Optimism: How to Change Your Mind and Your Life* (New York: Vintage, 2001).

3. L. B. Aknin et al., "Making a Difference Matters: Impact Unlocks the Emotional Benefits of Prosocial Spending," *Journal of Economic Behavior & Organization* 88 (2013): 90–95.

4. K. D. Smith, J. P. Keating, and E. Stotland, "Altruism Reconsidered: The Effect of Denying Feedback on a Victim's Status to Empathic Witnesses," *Journal of Personality and Social Psychology* 57, no. 4 (1989): 641.

5. K. Jenni and G. Loewenstein, "Explaining the Identifiable Victim Effect," *Journal of Risk and Uncertainty* 14, no. 3 (1997): 235–257; and D. A. Small and G. Loewenstein, "Helping a Victim or Helping the Victim: Altruism and Identifiability," *Journal of Risk and Uncertainty* 26, no. 1 (2003): 5–16.

6. A. M. Grant, "Does Intrinsic Motivation Fuel the Prosocial Fire? Motivational Synergy in Predicting Persistence, Performance, and Productivity," *Journal of Applied Psychology* 93, no. 1 (2008): 48; and A. M. Grant et al., "Impact and the Art of Motivation Maintenance: The Effects of Contact with Beneficiaries on Persistence Behavior," *Organizational Behavior and Human Decision Processes* 103, no. 1 (2007): 53–67.

7. A. M. Grant and F. Gino, "A Little Thanks Goes a Long Way: Explaining Why Gratitude Expressions Motivate Prosocial Behavior," *Journal of Personality and Social Psychology* 98, no. 6 (2010): 946.

8. A. M. Grant, "Leading with Meaning: Beneficiary Contact, Prosocial Impact, and the Performance Effects of Transformational Leadership," *Academy of Management Journal* 55, no. 2 (2012): 458–476.

9. K. Lanaj, R. E. Johnson, and M. Wang, "When Lending a Hand Depletes the Will: The Daily Costs and Benefits of Helping," *Journal of Applied Psychology* 101, no. 8 (2016): 1097.

Index

Acknowledgments

I just wrote a book about getting people to help you. And if you had any doubts about whether or not I am qualified to write that book, let me put those fears to rest right now. Because I have had *a lot* of help—so it stands to reason I know something about getting it, right?

For starters, I am, as always, grateful to my mother, Sigrid Grant, who has been my strongest supporter and most valuable adviser. She helps me with everything—and I mean everything—without me ever even *having* to ask. She's that good.

Speaking of being that good, thank you to my extraordinary editor-pretty-much-coauthor Sarah Green Carmichael. To say that she saved this book—and my sanity—is not even a tiny exaggeration. Her insights and guidance are everywhere, on every page. If you liked this book and found it useful, you have Sarah to thank for it.

I'm also grateful to the amazingly patient and encouraging Tim Sullivan, editorial director of the Harvard Business Review Press, who helped me shape the idea for the book and then waited without ever complaining even once for me to get around to writing the damn thing.

While I'm at it, a big thanks to everyone at HBR who has worked on this book and the ones before it.

This book, and every book I've ever written, owes the ultimate debt to my friend and rock star literary agent Giles Anderson. He is particularly gifted when it comes to telling which of my ideas are good and which are stinkers. He's batting 1000 so far. For making my career as an author possible, Giles, I thank you.

To my friends and colleagues who helped me shape the ideas in this book, who clued me into great research and stories, and pointed out all the things I might have missed, I thank: Drake Baer, Vanessa Bohns, Jay Dixit, Adam Grant (seriously, no relation), Tory Higgins, David Rock, Thomas Wedell-Wedellsborg, Tessa V. West, and Jay Van Bavel.

And on a personal note thank you, Joseph Francis, for always being the friend I need, in all the ways I need you to be. Somehow, you turned one of the hardest times in my life into one of the happiest ones.

Finally, I am grateful for my two children, Annika and Max. They didn't really help with the book, I'll be honest. But they make my life awesome.

About the Author

Heidi Grant, PhD, is Global Director of Research and Development at the NeuroLeadership Institute, and Associate Director of Columbia University's Motivation Science Center. She is the author of the international bestsellers *Nine Things Successful People Do Differently*, *Succeed: How We Can Reach Our Goals*, *No One Understands You and What to Do about It*, and *Focus: Use Different Ways of Seeing the World for Success and Influence* (with E. Tory Higgins).

She is a frequent contributor to *Harvard Business Review*, *strategy+business*, *Fast Company*, *99U*, *The Atlantic*, and *Psychology Today*, and has been listed as one of Thinkers50's top thought leaders in management.

Heidi earned her PhD from Columbia University, working with Carol Dweck (author of *Mindset: The New Psychology of Success*).

Heidi and her family live in Pelham, NY.

Visit her website: http://www.heidigrantphd.com/.